Car...

CITY LIMITS

Roadblocks Ahead

ROSITA J. DOZIER

Canaan
CITY LIMITS
Roadblocks Ahead

A Devotional Guide
to Overcoming the Giants
Blocking Our Entrance
to a Life of Abundance

ROSITA J. DOZIER

Canaan City Limits: Roadblocks Ahead

Trilogy Christian Publishers
A Wholly Owned Subsidiary of Trinity Broadcasting Network
2442 Michelle Drive, Tustin, CA 92780

Rights Department, 2442 Michelle Drive, Tustin, CA 92780.

Trilogy Christian Publishing/TBN and colophon are trademarks of Trinity Broadcasting Network.

For information about special discounts for bulk purchases, please contact Trilogy Christian Publishing.

Trilogy Disclaimer: The views and content expressed in this book are those of the author and may not necessarily reflect the views and doctrine of Trilogy Christian Publishing or the Trinity Broadcasting Network.

Manufactured in the United States of America
10 9 8 7 6 5 4 3 2 1
Library of Congress Cataloging-in-Publication Data is available.

ISBN: 979-8-88738-290-6
E-ISBN: 979-8-88738-291-3

Contents

The Beginning

We need to consider a few parallels to get a full picture of what the land of Canaan represents. God first appeared to Abram in Ur:

> *"Brothers and fathers, listen to me! The God of glory appeared to our father Abraham while he was still in Mesopotamia, before he lived in Haran. 'Leave your country and your people,' God said, 'and go to the land I will show you.'"*
>
> —Acts 7:2 NIV

The country was Ur, and it represents the place of the old life, the place of death and darkness. The old life is the place where we lived before God, where the Light of the World is revealed to us. Just as God called Abram out, He called the children of Israel out of Egypt. Egypt was a place of captivity and slavery, the place of their old life. God is still calling. Today, He calls the sinner to leave his residence since birth, the old life, the world of sin and death.

Abram also had to leave his family behind. His family (his kindred) represents the traditions of men. In the beginning, the Israelites did not want to leave Egypt; neither did Egypt want to let them go. Today's Christian must overcome the pull of this world's system, including family members, friends, co-workers, anyone around the believer who will try to keep them tied to their old ways.

Finally, God told Abram to leave his father's house. The father's house represents the old man—the nature of the first man, Adam. Abram's father had to die before he would leave. In like manner, the children of Israel had to leave the house of Pharaoh, the old life of slavery. Today's Christian must "put off the old self," the old man, which is corrupt (Ephesians 4:22 NIV).

> Terah took his son Abram, his grandson Lot son of Haran, and his daughter-in-law Sarai, the wife of his son Abram, and together they set out for Ur of the Chaldeans to go to Canaan. But when they came to Harran, they settled there. Terah lived 205 years, and he died in Harran.
>
> —Genesis 11:31–32 NIV

Abram was led out of Ur by his father, and on the way to Canaan, his father stopped in Harran. Harran was located between Ur and the land of Canaan. There is a lot of significance here. Terah settled for the middle ground. And because of Terah, Abram settled for less than the best. Abram did not fully obey God until his earthly father died.

Harran represents the outward appearance of godliness. It looked as though Abram had obeyed God, but in reality, he did not truly leave his father's house. Abram allowed his earthly father to take charge of his command to leave, thereby sacrificing his calling to come "out from among them." Abram lived seventy-five years in disobedience. It looked as if he had obeyed God because he left Ur, but in reality, he was out of the will of God.

The children of Israel were also sidetracked on their way to Canaan. Disobedience caused their forty-year wilderness wanderings. Christians today also get sidetracked on their way to Canaan. How often do we settle for second best and compromise? Our complete obedience to God's Word determines the length of time it takes us to get through the wilderness and arrive at the Land of Promise. Harran and the wilderness represent the wasted years of our lives. As long as we are disobeying God, there can be no fruit. And if we cannot produce fruit, then our lives are wasted (Matthew 3:10; 7:19 NIV; Luke 13:6–9 NIV).

Where are you currently living? Are you on the road to Canaan? Has the world, the flesh, and the devil sidetracked you? That place between the promise and the fulfillment of the promise is the wilderness. Your wilderness is the exact opposite of your promise.

Israel's promise was a land flowing with milk and honey. In their wilderness experience, they only had enough supply for each day: "The whole Israelite community set out from the Desert of Sin, traveling from place to place as the LORD commanded. They camped at Rephidim, but there was no water for the people to drink" (Exodus 17:1 NIV). Also, God fed them manna each day, but it was only enough for that day (Exodus 16:4, 18–20 NIV).

For forty years, Israel suffered in the wilderness because of unbelief. Fear kept them from obeying God. Only after they entered the Promised Land did God give them houses, and they did not build them (Deuteronomy 6:10–11 NIV). And only then did they have an abundance of food.

The intention of this devotional is to help you recognize the roadblocks that are keeping you on the outskirts of your promised land. Your time spent in the wilderness depends on your ability to believe God instead of being distracted by the roadblocks facing you outside the city limits of Canaan.

Canaan Land

Canaan was a land made up of seven nations. The inhabitants of these nations were known as the Canaanites, the Hittites, the Hivites, the Perizzites, the Girgashites, the Amorites, and the Jebusites. When Israelite spies were sent to investigate the land, they saw these people as giants. They later told Moses the Israelites would not be able to defeat the nations in the land. But God told the Israelites that He would drive out the inhabitants (Deuteronomy 7:1–2 KJV). Later, God told them to utterly destroy the inhabitants of the land (Deuteronomy 20:17 KJV). The few spies, however, were able to persuade the many Israelites not to believe God.

The names of these inhabitants of the land are especially important to this devotional study. The meaning of each name gives us a clue as to the stronghold each nation represents. As we understand each stronghold, we will see how they block our own entrance into the land that flows with milk and honey.

Each of these nations represents forces that people—Christians included—face every day. As we get into this study, you will see how these forces keep us from entering into our own Land of Promise. God desires that we overcome those forces and utterly destroy them.

Many of us see ourselves as "grasshoppers" (Numbers 13:33 NIV); not only that, but we believe others see us the same way. As a result, we never overcome the giants of depression, pride, fear, compromise, lack of discipline, and the flesh, and we never experience peace. If God has already chosen the land for us, as He did with the descendants of Abraham, then the giants are simply roadblocks. The roadblocks are barriers intended to deny us entrance into our inheritance.

Barriers prevent us from reaching a goal. Whether it is positive or negative, the barriers are intended to prevent. Oftentimes, that goal is very valuable to us. In the case of Israel, the land was their inheritance, and the goal of the giants was to keep the abundant land for themselves. Unfortunately for them, God promised the land flowing with milk and honey to Abraham, the father of all who believe (Romans 4:12 NIV). In the case of today's Christian, Jesus came to give us abundant life. That abundant life is dependent on our ability to overcome the giants facing us each day, as well as our obedience to the Word that comes out of the mouth of God, the Bible.

Let us take a closer look at the inhabitants of the Promised Land and identify the roadblock each nation represents. As I mentioned earlier, the meaning of each nation's name gives us insight into its power.

GIANT	ROADBLOCK
Canaanites	*Low self-esteem*
Hittites	*Fear*
Girgashites	*Carnality*
Amorites	*Pride*
Hivites	*Compromise*
Jebusites	*Lack of peace*
Perizzites	*Lack of discipline*

This book, *Canaan City Limits: Roadblocks Ahead*, was written for the believer who wants to possess/own the land as

God intended them to do. To have life is good, but to have life more abundantly is better. These seven nations have survived because Israel did not obey God to the letter. To experience all that God has for us, we must "utterly destroy" the giants that block our path to abundant living.

The number *seven* has great significance in Scripture. Seven is the number of temporal perfection or completion. The root meaning of the word *seven* is "full or satisfied, to have enough." On the seventh day, God rested from His labor, the work of creation. As we overcome these seven giants, we can enter a temporary rest. This rest is temporary because each day is new, and giants are always on the horizon. Pray for wisdom to recognize and destroy the roadblocks to your inheritance.

Revelation 2 and 3 reveal promises to those believers who overcome. There is a message to the overcomer. Will you have ears to hear what the Spirit is saying to you?

Main Scripture References

They came back to Moses and Aaron and the whole Israelite community at Kadesh in the Desert of Paran. There they reported to them and to the whole assembly and showed them the fruit of the land. They gave Moses this account: "We went into the land to which you sent us, and it does flow with milk and honey! Here is its fruit. But the people who live there are powerful, and the cities are fortified and very large. We even saw descendants of Anak there."

—Numbers 13:26–28 NIV

"When the LORD your God brings you into the land you are entering to possess and drives out before you many nations—the Hittites, Girgashites, Amorites, Canaanites, Perizzites, Hivites and Jebusites, seven nations larger and stronger than you—and when the LORD your God has delivered them over to you and you have defeated them, you must destroy them totally. Make no treaty with them, and show them no mercy."

—Deuteronomy 7:1–2 NIV

"This is how you will know that the living God is among you and that he will certainly drive out before you the Canaanites, Hittites, Hivites, Perizzites, Girgashites, Amorites and Jebusites."

—Joshua 3:10 NIV

MEANINGS OF WORDS, KEYED TO *STRONG'S CONCORDANCE*

- *Canaanite* *(3669) dwell in the valley, bring down low
- *Amorites* *(567) highlander, mountaineer
- *Jebusites* *(2983) (2982) trodden, threshing, polluted
- *Hivites* *(2340) villager, encampment
- *Perizzites* *(6522) unwalled
- *Hittites* *(2850) terror, to breakdown, discourage
- *Girgashites* *(1622) earthly, clay pot

The Message to the Overcomer is a collection of messages written to encourage Christians to experience a deeper life in Christ. Each message offers a practical approach to overcoming life's issues. As we apply the word in our lives, we will begin experiencing the overcoming life. My desire is to see God's people grow in grace and in the knowledge of the Lord Jesus Christ. "And they overcame him by the blood of the Lamb and by the word of their testimony, and they did not love their lives to the death." Revelation 12:11 KJV

Roadblocks to Your Promise

We face the same challenges as the Israelites did on the way to their promise. The world, the flesh, and the devil are the major roadblocks we face daily.

Their first and the biggest challenge was Pharaoh, the ruler of Egypt (the world). After finally agreeing to let the Israelites go with Moses, he began to regret his decision (Exodus 14:5–8 NIV) Pharaoh pursued the Israelites, hoping to get them back so they could continue to serve him and the Egyptian nation. The world may eventually let you go, but it will then pursue you in the effort to enslave you again. The world will remind you of what you used to be and what you used to do, and it will never stop pursuing you. So, the "Pharaoh systems" of this world are major roadblocks to your promise.

Roadblock number two is that Philistine (giant) talking to you. What are you hearing? To what are you listening? In 1 Samuel 17:1–11 (NIV), Goliath was tormenting Israel with his words. The men of Israel were afraid, and they ran. Then David came along and did not let the words of the Philistine intimidate him. He refused to hear the words of the giant; David maintained his focus on the Lord. We, in turn, should learn from David. Ignore the words of the giants. Do not listen to the negative report of sickness and disease. Overcome that roadblock of flesh with the encouraging words of the Spirit. God's Word is spirit and life.

The third major roadblock is the thief. He comes to steal, kill, and destroy. We know the thief as Satan, the father of lies. He will use any means to keep us out of the will of God. Your entrance into the promise is God's will for your life. Therefore, resist the enemy (James 4:7 NIV), and he will flee. Jesus resisted the words of Satan with the Word of God, and He eventually returned to His estate in heaven. Adam and Eve acquiesced to the words of Satan and doubted God's instructions. Therefore, they were expelled from the Garden.

This roadblock is meant to keep you from entering the Land of Promise, the land of abundance. Although the land is already yours, the enemy is preparing for your arrival. To conquer Canaan and its many avenues, your flesh must be made subject to God. If you question God's Word, your Promised Land will remain elusive, and the roadblocks will accomplish their goal: to keep you away from your abundant life.

Nothing has changed; the enemy's tactics are still the same today. Ecclesiastes 1:9 tells us: "What has been will be again, what has been done will be done again; there is nothing new under the sun" (NIV). The enemy is still trying to bring division between you and your God, between you and the Lord Jesus Christ.

SECTION 1
The Giant of Fear

- HITTITE: The giant of fear
- DEFINITION: Terror, apprehension, to be in awe of, a lack of faith, dread
- SOLUTION: Stand fast in faith (1 Corinthians 16:13 KJV)

MESSAGE TO THE OVERCOMER

"The LORD is on my side; I will not fear: what can man do unto me?"

—Psalm 118:6 KJV

Fear is very debilitating. With fear comes torment (1 John 4:18 KJV). Have you ever been so afraid that you could not move? Or have you been so afraid that you began to make a list of all the things that could go wrong? Fear has a way of stifling our creativity. It has a way of stopping our progress. Fear has the power to change lives—and not for the better.

Society classifies various types of fear, and through it, fear has a name. That name is *phobia*, meaning "the fear of." Some well-known phobias include the fear of flying, the fear of crowds, and the fear of failure. No matter the name, fear hinders us from doing what we should do and being who we really are.

The Bible mentions many different kinds of fear. There is the fear of death (Genesis 21:17 KJV; Hebrews 2:15 KJV); the fear of danger (Exodus 14:13 KJV); the fear of nothing, or imaginative fear (Psalm 53:5 KJV); the fear of war (Psalm 27:3 KJV); the fear of evil (Psalm 23:4 KJV; Proverbs 1:33 KJV); and the fear of dreams (Job 4:13–14 NIV), just to name a few.

Fear is not new. The enemy still uses fear to stop the child of God from being all that he or she can be for Him. It is time to rise and overcome that giant of fear; it is time to possess the land that God has given to you. It is time to destroy that roadblock to your success. The time has come to exchange fear for faith.

Faith is the opposite of fear. When fear grips your heart, that is a sure sign it is time for faith to take over. No matter the situation, faith is the answer to fear. Trust in God is what you need when the fear of flying faces you. Trust in God's ability is what you need when the fear of failure is staring you in the face.

I remember an incident when I was forced to reconcile within myself the Scripture that says, "Fear hath torment" (1 John 4:18 KJV). I started living in a house that had been vacant for a while, and it was in pretty bad shape. There were holes in the ceilings and the walls, and the house had rodents. I planned to repair the house, and in order to do so, I needed to live in it.

The room I chose to sleep in had a large hole in the ceiling. The hole was on the opposite wall from my bed. The kitchen was next to the room in which I was sleeping, and it had several large holes in the ceiling and walls, as well. One night, while in the kitchen, I was frightened when a huge rat jumped from the wall into the ceiling. Yes, it was huge, with a very long tail. I thought, *That is no mouse!* It turned out to be a field rat from the grassy area behind the house.

Needless to say, I could not sleep that night. All I could think about was the hole in the ceiling, in the room where I was trying to sleep. My soul was tormented as I imagined what could happen. Every sound, every movement, any little noise had me on edge. It was like that for many nights. Finally, the Lord spoke to my heart and said, *Fear has torment.*

What a way to experience the Word! I began to pray for peace. I prayed for the faith to trust God to care for me and not allow rats, mice, or anything else to harm me. I will never forget that time, when my fear turned into faith. I had to trust in God and His power to protect me and keep me safe. The solution to overcoming the giant of fear is to stand fast in faith, to be courageous, and to be strong (1 Corinthians 16:13).

DAY ONE
Be Strong in Faith

He staggered not at the promise of God through unbelief;
but was strong in faith, giving glory to God; and being
fully persuaded that, what he had promised, he was able
also to perform.

—Romans 4:20–21 KJV

To overcome fear, we must be strong in faith. When we are answering the call of God to conquer, fear has a way of creeping up on us. It does not matter how strong we are in the Word; fear will always come to visit, hoping to find a home. Its goal is to cause us to fail and to disobey God.

Has God given you a promise? What stopped you from experiencing the fulfillment of that promise? No matter the name you give it, it always boils down to fear. The only solution to fear is to "stand fast in the faith" (1 Corinthians 16:13 KJV). To stand fast in faith, we must believe what God says to us.

The voice of God is the basis of our faith. When we are facing circumstances in life, a word from God is what gives us direction. Abraham initially took note of his natural situation when God promised him a son. Eventually, he entered a different realm by choosing not to consider his natural circumstances.

So it is for us. We are so accustomed to living according to what we see, feel, taste, touch, and hear—all that is the flesh—and we are very much in tune with it. When we decide to live by the Word of God, something happens inside of us. The Scriptures call it a "struggle" between the flesh and the spirit.

The flesh will make decisions for us until we start choosing God's way. Thus, the battle begins for control of the body. It happens; it happened with Abram. He and Sarai decided to help God out. The flesh was tired of waiting, so Sarai made a suggestion and Ishmael was born (Genesis 16:1–16 KJV). The name *Ishmael* means "God hears."

Standing strong in faith requires us to make certain choices. Every day our choice is to let the Spirit guide us, and then we must choose to go where the Spirit leads. Hearing from God and doing what He says to do is the key to being strong in faith. Strong in faith does not mean being idle. *Faith* is an action word: "Faith, if it hath not works is dead, being alone" (James 2:14–17 KJV). Being strong in faith simply means that if we believe, then we are acting in accordance with what we believe. Work follows faith. We will never be strong in faith without action.

We all suffer from the "I'm not sure if it's God" syndrome. If it sounds like God, if it feels like God, if it is something that God would do, then by faith, just do it—to the glory of God! He has a way of letting us know whether we are about to miss the mark if we just listen.

PRAYER

Father,

Thank You for an overcoming spirit. Thank You for mustard-seed faith (Luke 17:5–6 KJV), which moves mountains. Thank You for the shield of faith (Ephesians 6:16 KJV), which blocks the fiery darts of the enemy.

I know that without faith, it is impossible to please You, and if I live in fear, then I live in sin (Romans 14:23 KJV). So, Lord, thank You for reminding me to walk by faith and to live by faith.

In Jesus' name, amen.

REFLECTIONS

In what areas of your life is fear a problem?

_____

_____

_____

_____

_____

_____

_____

_____

_____

_____

_____

_____

Canaan City Limits: Roadblocks Ahead

LIFE APPLICATION

What will you start doing today to demonstrate your faith?

_____

_____

_____

_____

_____

_____

_____

_____

_____

_____

_____

_____

_____

_____

_____

_____

_____

_____

_____

_____

_____

NOTES

DAY TWO
Live by Faith

Now the just shall live by faith.

—Hebrews 10:38 KJV

The just means *you*, if you have been washed in the blood of Jesus, if you have accepted Him as your Savior and Lord. Jesus makes us righteous, holy, and just. Because of that, we can live by faith. This simply means that all we do in life we do trusting and believing God. No matter how small or how large, faith should motivate everything we do. Faith is trusting God, fully persuaded that He can care for us, to meet our needs, no matter what they are. Faith is the full assurance of God's ability. When we are weak, then God can be strong in us, and for us (2 Corinthians 12:10 KJV).

The stronghold of fear is a major hindrance to obeying God—or should I say, obeying the voice of God. So many times, I would hear the voice of God speaking to me, but fear would stop me from responding to His voice. Do you know what I mean? *Is that really God, or is it me? Lord, if that is really You, then give me a confirmation sign.* Fear has just taken over your relationship with your heavenly Father.

So often I would not do what God was saying because I was not sure whether He was speaking to me. Fear would overtake me and paralyze me. Whatever else was going on at the time I missed, because of fear.

God had to teach me a lesson. Many times, God would tell me to go and pray for a certain person. I would be gripped with fear, all the while petitioning God for confirmation. God began giving me confirmation by sending someone else to do the job He had asked *me* to do. I would feel so bad—like a failure—when that would happen. I had failed God! But it did not matter how bad I felt, I failed God over and over. Finally, one day I put two and two together. Whenever God spoke to me to act, the enemy would bring fear to stop me. Slowly I began to use that fear as a green light instead of a red light. I began to step out in faith, knees wobbling, hands shaking, and voice trembling, but answering the call of God.

PRAYER

Father,

    In the name of Jesus, thank You for teaching me how to live by faith. Thank You for showing me how to trust You in every situation, knowing that You are leading and guiding me into all truth and righteousness. Thank You for never failing me, even though I often fail You.

    You are Jehovah Shammah, the God who is always present. Thank You. Amen.

REFLECTIONS

What have you discovered about faith and fear?

_____

_____

_____

_____

_____

_____

_____

_____

_____

_____

_____

_____

_____

_____

_____

_____

_____

_____

_____

_____

_____

LIFE APPLICATION

What can you do today to exercise your faith in a greater way?

_____

_____

_____

_____

_____

_____

_____

_____

_____

_____

_____

_____

_____

_____

_____

_____

_____

_____

_____

_____

NOTES

DAY THREE
Love Never Fails

For God hath not given us the spirit of fear; but of power, and of love, and of a sound mind.
—2 Timothy 1:7 KJV

Let's examine this Scripture closely. The word "power," *dunamis* in the Greek, means "ability." Therefore, we see that God's Spirit brings ability and might. The spirit of the enemy brings fear. Remember, we are still overcoming the giant of fear. The Amplified Bible says it this way: "For God has not given us a spirit of timidity, of cowardice, of craven and cringing and fawning fear, but He has given us a spirit of power and of love and of calm and well-balanced mind and discipline and self-control."

To overcome the giant of fear, we must recognize which spirit is at work (1 John 4:1 KJV). The phrase "sound mind" means to have self-control. When situations and circumstances do not rattle you, then you have control of your mind. Having control of your mind also means not allowing yourself to think of all the things that could go wrong. Murphy's Law is a good example of fear being in control: "Anything that could go wrong will go wrong." You find yourself expecting something bad to happen. Guess what? Something negative will happen. The spiritual mind does not dwell on the natural life.

The spiritual mind takes notice of the spiritual realm, discerning the spirits at work.

The Spirit of God is also love. The word "love" comes from the Greek word *agape*. *Agape* is a verb, an action word. Therefore, the Spirit of love causes one to act. Love never fails, because *agape* is not based on what someone does or does not do for you. *Agape* is selfless love. Unconditional love moves you in the direction of God. So, when fear pops up its ugly head, its intention is to prevent you from moving. Can you see this? Fear causes red lights to go off, but love turns on the green light. Fear and love cannot operate at the same time. One or the other will control your life. Choose this day to whom you will give yourself.

PRAYER

Father,

In the name of Jesus, thank You for giving me Your Spirit. Thank You that I do not have to live in fear or allow the spirit of fear to hinder the work to which You have called me.

Your love controls my life, and because of that, I know when You are at work in my life and when the enemy of my soul is looking to devour me.

Thank You, Father, for Your unconditional love toward me. Thank You for showing me how to love others.

You, O Lord, are in the midst of all that I do. Amen.

REFLECTION

In what area (s) of your life has God's love been absent?

_____

_____

_____

_____

_____

_____

_____

_____

_____

_____

_____

_____

_____

_____

_____

_____

_____

_____

LIFE APPLICATION

What are your thoughts concerning the love of God being used as a weapon against fear?

_____

_____

_____

_____

_____

_____

_____

_____

_____

_____

_____

_____

_____

_____

_____

_____

_____

_____

_____

_____

_____

_____

NOTES

DAY FOUR
By Faith

*By faith we understand the worlds... were framed
(fashioned, put in order and equipped for their intended
purpose) by the word of God, so that what we see was
not made out of things which are visible.*

—Hebrews 11:3 AMPC

By faith, all things are possible. Even faith as a grain of mustard seed is powerful (Matthew 17:20 KJV). Faith is the mechanism used to create. By faith God created the worlds (the universe) with His own words. He did not see an example of what He wanted to make; He did not see a blueprint other than what was in His mind. He framed the universe and decided what it would look like; He put everything in order, setting up the universe, equipping it for its intended purpose, and giving it everything it needed to operate. This happened, all by faith, before it was seen.

Overcoming the giant of fear takes faith. The opposite of fear is faith. Fear tells us that overcoming is not possible. Fear is a flesh product and is in total opposition to the Spirit. "Walk in the Spirit and ye shall not fulfill the lust of the flesh" (Galatians 5:16 KJV). The giant of fear is always before us, always facing us down concerning our entrance into the Promised Land. This giant is prominent in everyday life and is the most difficult giant to overcome. But whenever you recognize fear, that is the time to act. That is the time to make the choice to walk by faith.

Living by faith can be an expression of your words. In Luke 7:6–7 a man whose servant was ill said to Jesus, "Lord, don't trouble yourself, for I do not deserve to have you come under my roof. That is why I did not even consider myself worthy to come to you. But say the word, and my servant will be healed" (NIV). Jesus called this "great faith."

Living by faith can be an action. In Matthew 14:36, all who were diseased were taken to Jesus: "And besought him that they might only touch the hem of his garment: and as many as touched were made perfectly whole" (KJV). Of course, we know the story of the woman who touched the hem of Jesus' garment and was healed (Mark 5:34 NIV).

Living by faith in Jesus is the key. All these examples demonstrate the faith each of these people had in Jesus. If they could only get to Jesus or if they could only speak a word to Him, He solved their problems. By faith you can overcome any giant, and the giant of fear is no different. Just get to Jesus.

PRAYER

Father,

Thank You for being the God who heals and delivers. Thank You for Your lovingkindness, Your grace, and Your mercy. Thank You for showing me how to increase my faith to overcome the spirit of fear.

Thank You for Your Word, which says "by faith"—by faith, I can create a life of abundance; by faith, I can overcome the giant called fear; by faith, I will enter the Land of Promise. Thank You, Lord, for Your encouragement, found in the Word of God. By faith, I will knock down the roadblocks that seek to keep me away from my promise.

In Jesus' name, amen.

REFLECTIONS

What part of this section stood out for you?

_____

_____

_____

_____

_____

_____

_____

_____

_____

_____

LIFE APPLICATION

What did you learn about the phrase "by faith," and how can you make it a part of your vocabulary?

_____

_____

_____

_____

_____

_____

_____

_____

_____

_____

_____

_____

_____

_____

_____

_____

_____

_____

_____

_____

_____

_____

_____

NOTES

SECTION 2
The Giant of Carnality

- GIRGASHITE: The giant of carnality
- DEFINITION: Flesh, self, soul (emotion, mind, will)
- SOLUTION: Walk in the Spirit (Galatians 5:16 KJV)

MESSAGE TO THE OVERCOMER

"For if you live according to [the dictates of] the flesh, you will surely die. But if through the power of the [Holy] Spirit you are [habitually] putting to death (making extinct, deadening) the [evil] deeds prompted by the body, you shall [really and genuinely] live forever."

—Romans 8:13 AMPC

That old saying "man is his own worst enemy" is so true. One of the biggest giants we face on the road to the Land of Promise is "self," better known as "the flesh." "Flesh" in the Bible points to all that an unregenerated person is. The flesh senses the world around it; thus, a person who follows the world walks after the flesh. The flesh makes "self" the center and elevates self-will above God's will.

Man's initial fall, in the Garden of Eden, was the result of Adam's soul (his emotions, mind, will) resisting the authority of his spirit. As a result, man became enslaved to the body and its passions. In essence, man's spirit became a prisoner. Man is now a fleshly being, no longer under the Spirit's control (spiritual). The soul is now under the power of the flesh.

To be born into this world is to be born of the flesh. It would naturally hold true that we are free of the flesh through death: "For he that is dead is freed from sin" (Romans 6:7 KJV); "I am crucified with Christ: nevertheless I live; yet not I, but Christ liveth in me" (Galatians 2:20 KJV). The only way to walk in the Spirit is to crucify the deeds of the body. The believer's flesh is crucified with Christ on the cross. We need only apply, by the Holy Spirit, the power of the Lord's death. We do not need to crucify the flesh again and again. We need to choose to walk in the Spirit and not fulfill the lusts of the flesh. To walk in the Spirit is to allow the Spirit to lead us and do what He is telling us to do.

In Romans 8:13 (KJV), the apostle Paul was not advocating the suppression of all physical desires or the denial of any enjoyment of physical pleasure. He is saying that all bodily activity executed independently of the Spirit should be put to death. We believers are not obligated to respond to the flesh. The purpose of God is not to reform the flesh, but to destroy it. The Bible mentions no other ways of dealing with the flesh. The only method of deliverance is death. The blood of Jesus washes away our sins—but not our flesh. The flesh is ordained to die.

Whenever we equate ourselves with the flesh by saying, "My temper is really bad," or "I'm just a sinner," or "I can't help myself," we are giving in to the power of the flesh. When the flesh demands to exert itself, if, at that moment, we agree with what God says about us, we can experience deliverance. According to God's Word, our flesh is crucified with Christ. We agree with this by saying, "Yes, Lord! Indeed, my flesh is crucified with Christ." We must never allow our experience to override what God's Word says about us. If God says so, then that settles it.

For they that are after the flesh do mind the things of the flesh; but they that are after the Spirit the things of the Spirit. For to be carnally minded is death; but to be spiritually minded is life and peace.
—Romans 8:5–6 KJV

Those who live according to the flesh have their minds set on what the flesh desires; but those who live in accordance with the Spirit have their minds set on what the Spirit desires. The mind governed by the flesh is death, but the mind governed by the Spirit is life and peace.
—Romans 8:5–6 NIV

DAY ONE
The Deeds of the Flesh

*Now the works of the flesh are manifest, which are
these; adultery, fornication, uncleanness, lasciviousness,
idolatry, witchcraft, hatred, variance, emulation, wrath,
strife, seditions, heresies, envyings, murders, drunkenness, revellings, and such like.*
　　　　　　　　　　　　—Galatians 5:19–21 KJV

The Amplified Bible starts this verse by saying, "Now the
doings (practices) of the flesh are clear" (AMPC). The J.B.
Phillips translation says it this way: "The activities of the lower
nature are obvious." Whatever translation you use, the meaning
is the same: The flesh does not produce good fruit. The flesh
cannot produce any good thing. No wonder Romans 8:13 tells
us to "put to death the misdeeds of the body" (NIV).

The "misdeeds" of the flesh have five groups:

- *Sins that defile the body:* immorality, impurity,
  licentiousness
- *Sinful communications with satanic forces:* idolatry,
  sorcery (witchcraft)
- *Sinful temper:* enmity (hatred), strife, jealousy,
  anger
- *Religious sects:* selfishness, dissensions, envy, party
  spirit
- *Lasciviousness*: drunkenness, carousing

The works of the flesh are no mystery. We all understand them, oh so well. The main issue is knowing how *not* to act in such ways. We are overly concerned with the works of the flesh, while God is concerned with the flesh itself. We tend to focus on the sin, which is the fruit of the flesh. God's focus is on the flesh itself, which is the root cause of sinful fruit.

If we want the Holy Spirit to lead us and set us free from the oppression of the flesh, we must put to death the wicked deeds of the body (Romans 8:13 NIV). When we do not follow the Holy Spirit, we immediately revert to following the flesh, serving sin (Romans 7:25 NIV). Therefore, it takes constant vigilance, both to obey God's voice and to be willing to put to death the deeds of the body. Notice, we are told to put to death the *deeds* of the flesh. We can utterly destroy all of the giants except the Girgashite. The natural man will always be with us. Therefore, we must put to death, or die to self, daily.

Because we are destined to live in these fleshly vessels, the flesh giant will always show up on our road to the Land of Promise. This giant knows that as long as he has his way, you will never reach your full potential. This giant's aim is to keep you focused on the world. He wants to keep you fighting for your life, when, in fact, death is actually your access to the abundant life. What a contradiction! Death brings life. It worked for Jesus, and it will work for you, as well.

PRAYER

Father,

You want us to follow after You. Thank You for the will to agree with You rather than with my flesh.

Now I understand why the flesh has been crucified

with Christ. There is no good thing in the flesh, according to Romans 7:18. I pray that all my actions are motivated by Your Spirit.

Thank You for helping me understand how to overcome this roadblock to abundant life, which is in Christ Jesus. Amen.

REFLECTIONS

What has God revealed to you while reading this section?

_____

_____

_____

_____

_____

_____

_____

_____

_____

_____

_____

_____

_____

_____

_____

_____

_____

_____

_____

_____

LIFE APPLICATION

What are your thoughts concerning the deeds of the flesh and their groups?

_____

_____

_____

_____

_____

_____

_____

_____

_____

_____

_____

_____

_____

_____

_____

_____

_____

_____

_____

_____

_____

NOTES

DAY TWO
No Confidence in the Flesh

For we are the circumcision, which worship God in the spirit, and rejoice in Christ Jesus, and have no confidence in the flesh.

—Philippians 3:3 KJV

Unless we are ready to deny all flesh—bad and good—we cannot walk in the Spirit, be pleasing to God, and live a genuine spiritual life.

Whether good flesh or bad, flesh is flesh. We are to put no confidence in the flesh, including my flesh, your flesh, your son's flesh, your daughter's flesh, your husband's flesh, the preacher's flesh, good old Charlie's flesh, anybody's flesh. Have I made my point?

In the J.B. Phillips translation of 2 Corinthians 5:16, Paul states, "Our knowledge of men can no longer be based on their outward lives (indeed, even though we knew Christ as a man we do not know him like that any longer)."

Keep in mind that the term *flesh* covers everything human. Whatever is natural is not spiritual. We must deny the wicked deeds of the flesh, but we must also deny our own righteousness and our own wisdom, any of our own honorable deeds not initiated by the Spirit. Unless we daily experience death and allow the Holy Spirit to have control of our bodies, we will never overcome the flesh giant.

It is hard to give up the right to be our own person—unless we realize that being our own person keeps us from being close to God. And unless we are close to God, we will never taste the grapes that await us in the Land of Promise. Unless we put to death *all* the deeds of the flesh, we will continue to live off the wilderness provision, which is just enough for today. And we will never enter into our own Promised Land.

No matter how much the mind may want to serve God's Law, the flesh will always want to serve sin. Serving God with my mind means to desire what God desires. Serving sin with my flesh means wanting what the flesh desires. Every moment of the day, a choice has to be made: Will I walk in the Spirit, or will I fulfill the lust of the flesh?

PRAYER

Father,

Thank You that I know and understand there is no good thing in the flesh. Because of that, I will not put my confidence in it. Thank You that I am a spiritual being, although the natural life is in conflict with that. Thank You for the power and the ability to overcome the flesh and live the life You have called me to live.

Father, knowing that there is no good thing in the flesh, I will choose to walk in the Spirit. Though it is hard sometimes to accept, flesh is flesh, and no matter how good a person is, without Christ Jesus as their Savior, their good works will never glorify You. I want to glorify You. In Jesus' name, amen.

REFLECTIONS

What did the Spirit of God reveal to you about putting your confidence in the flesh?

_____

_____

_____

_____

_____

_____

_____

_____

_____

_____

_____

_____

_____

_____

_____

_____

_____

_____

_____

LIFE APPLICATION

What can you do today to deny your flesh and live according to the Spirit?

_____

_____

_____

_____

_____

_____

_____

_____

_____

_____

_____

_____

_____

_____

_____

_____

_____

_____

_____

NOTES

DAY THREE
Abstain from Fleshly Lusts

*Dearly beloved, I beseech you as strangers and pilgrims,
abstain from fleshly lusts, which war against the soul.*
—1 Peter 2:11 KJV

*Dear friends, I beg you, you are only visitors here on
earth for a short time. Put away human evil desires.
These things make war with the soul.*
—1 Peter 2:11 (Simple English Bible)

According to the King James Version, 1 Peter 2:11 tells us to "abstain from fleshly lusts," while the Simple English Bible instructs us to "put away human evil desires." Lust is the same as desire, but lust has a negative connotation. Lust is what leads us into sin.

*Every man is tempted, when he is drawn away of his
own lust, and enticed. Then when lust hath conceived, it
bringeth forth sin: and sin, when it is finished, bringeth
forth death.*
—James 1:14–15 KJV

From whence come wars and fightings among you?
come they not hence, even of your lusts that war in your
members? Ye lust, and have not: ye kill, and desire to
have, and cannot obtain.

—James 4:1–2 KJV

No wonder Peter tells us to abstain from fleshly lust. The word *abstain* means "to restrain oneself from doing or enjoying something, to choose not to do something." It is a decision we must make, a decision not to let ourselves be drawn away by the appetites of the flesh. First Peter gives us several reasons to abstain from fleshly lusts. The first reason is because we are pilgrims, or visitors, here on the earth. We should not get caught up with what this world offers because this place is not our home. "Our citizenship is in heaven. And we eagerly await a Savior from there, the Lord Jesus Christ" (Philippians 3:20 NIV).

Our bodies are what ties us to the earth. Therefore, we are naturally drawn to what the world has to offer: "For all that is in the world, the lust of the flesh, and the lust of the eyes and the pride of life, is not of the Father, but is of the world. And the world passeth away, and the lust thereof" (1 John 2:16 KJV).

Another reason to abstain from fleshly lusts is because lust makes war with the soul. Man is comprised of a body, a soul, and a spirit. The soul provides self-awareness; the body is aware of its surroundings (the world); and the spirit allows us to experience God-awareness. The soul consists of the emotions, the mind, and the will. Our emotions express how we feel; the mind tells us what to think; and the will communicates what we want. The will is the decision-making part of us.

The mind is the most important part of us in this scenario: "As [a man] thinketh in his heart, so is he" (Proverbs 23:7 KJV). No wonder we need to renew the mind (Romans 12:2 KJV; Ephesians 4:23 KJV). We need to think on spiritual things, good things (Philippians 4:8 KJV). The soul is sandwiched between the spirit and the body. The soul will gravitate either toward the spirit or toward the body, depending on which is the strongest. If the spirit man is strong, then the emotions, the will, and the mind will respond to the dictates of the spirit. The same holds true for the body. If your body is in control, then the soul will do whatever the body wants to do. Remember, the body constantly relates to the world. This is the crux of the Christian life: to walk in the Spirit or walk in the flesh (Romans 8:4–5 KJV).

The solution to abstaining from fleshly lusts is found in Galatians 5:16: "This I say then, Walk in the Spirit and ye shall not fulfill the lust of the flesh" (KJV). Every minute of the day, we make choices, either for the spirit or for the flesh. The change can happen when the mind is renewed by the Word of God, which strengthens our spirits. Then we can make the choice to walk in the Spirit and be led by the spirit.

PRAYER

Father,

Thank You for loving me so much that You have warned me about fleshly lusts. Thank You for helping me understand what lust is and how it wars against my soul. Thank You that I am now able to recognize the warfare between my soul and my spirit and their desire to control my body and run my life.

Thank You, Father, and thank You, Lord, for being the power that lives in me and gives me the ability to overcome the pull of the world through lust. The lust of the eyes—wanting what I see—no longer has the power to motivate my actions. The pride of life—the desire for power and fame—has no control over me. I am content with what I have. The lust of the flesh—physical pleasure—is a constant battle, but my desire is to walk in the Spirit so that I will not fulfill the lusts of the flesh.

Thank You, Father, for Your Word, which heals and delivers, and I am blessed to know how to live according to Your Word.

In Jesus' name, amen.

REFLECTIONS

What in this section stood out the most to you?

_____

_____

_____

_____

_____

_____

_____

_____

_____

_____

_____

LIFE APPLICATION

What can you do today to abstain from fleshly lust?

_____

_____

_____

_____

_____

_____

_____

_____

_____

_____

_____

_____

_____

_____

_____

_____

_____

_____

_____

_____

NOTES

_____

_____

_____

_____

_____

_____

_____

_____

_____

_____

_____

_____

_____

_____

_____

_____

_____

_____

_____

_____

_____

_____

_____

DAY FOUR
Do God's Will

Therefore, since Christ suffered for us in the flesh, arm yourselves also with the same mind, for he who has suffered in the flesh has ceased from sin, that he no longer should live the rest of his time in the flesh for the lusts of men, but for the will of God.

—1 Peter 4:1–2 NIV

I hope you have a better understanding of the giant of carnality that blocks your entrance into a life in the Spirit. *Carnality* simply means "fleshly lusts." Remember, the flesh wars against the spirit. The flesh cares nothing about letting the spirit lead. Your Land of Promise is a life that is Spirit-led, in which you hear the voice of the Lord, but you cannot be led if you will not follow: "And the world passeth away, and the lust thereof: but he that doeth the will of God abideth forever" (1 John 2:17 KJV).

Let us look at the will of God concerning your body. Second Corinthians 7:1 states: "Dearly beloved, let us cleanse ourselves from all filthiness of the flesh and spirit, perfecting holiness in the fear of God" (KJV). The word *filthiness* means "defilement." In other words, we must cleanse ourselves from all defilement of our bodies and spirits. *Perfection* means "to bring to completion." *Holiness* is the "quality of sanctification."

We should have our inner being and outward man so permeated by the Holy Spirit that it *all* becomes holy. This is the will of God for you.

> *For ye are bought with a price: therefore glorify God in your body, and in your spirit, which are God's.*
> —1 Corinthians 6:20 KJV

> *Be not conformed to this world: but be ye transformed by the renewing of your mind, that ye may prove what is that good, and acceptable, and perfect, will of God.*
> —Romans 12:2 KJV

> *I beseech you therefore, brethren, by the mercies of God, that ye present your bodies a living sacrifice, holy, acceptable unto God, which is your reasonable service.*
> —Romans 12:1 KJV

PRAYER

Father,

In the name of Jesus, I thank You for this study. I want to do Your will in my life. I want the Spirit to lead me in all that I do. Encourage me to be willing when I am not.

Thanks for letting me see You in every situation of life. Thank You for being concerned about my growth and maturity.

I love You. Amen.

REFLECTIONS

How does doing the will of God help to abstain from fleshy lust?

_____

_____

_____

_____

_____

_____

_____

_____

_____

_____

_____

_____

_____

_____

_____

_____

_____

_____

_____

LIFE APPLICATION

What can you do today to line up with the Word of God concerning His will for your body?

_____

_____

_____

_____

_____

_____

_____

_____

_____

_____

_____

_____

_____

_____

_____

_____

_____

_____

NOTES

SECTION 3
The Giant of Discouragement

- JEBUSITE: The giant called lack of peace, or discouragement
- DEFINITION: Agitation, disturbance, polluted
- SOLUTION: Peace of God (Philippians 4:7 KJV)

MESSAGE TO THE OVERCOMER

And let the peace of God rule in your hearts, to the which also ye are called in one body; and be ye thankful.

—Colossians 3:15 KJV

Two things stand out to me in this verse of Scripture. First, it says we are called to peace, and second, it tells us that peace is a by-product of being thankful. When we exercise thanksgiving, discouragement is nowhere to be found. Praise and thanksgiving for all we have, or even what we do not have, brings a spirit of contentment. Philippians 4:11–13 (KJV) speaks of being content in whatever situation or state we find ourselves. Thanksgiving leads to the peace of God, which will then flow from us to others.

What does it mean "to be called to peace"? We are called to live in peace (Romans 12:18 KJV). We know how difficult it is to be at peace with everyone. But God says that as much as it lies within you, we should live in peace with all men. The only way we can do that is to have the peace of God living in us. Of course, we need to be Christians first. Without Christ living in us, peace is extremely hard to come by.

The most important fact concerning the peace of God is that there is no peace *of* God without peace *with* God. We will touch on peace with God a little later in this section. The solution to not having peace is to know the peace of God.

The peace of God has many benefits:

And the peace of God, which transcends all understanding, will guard your hearts and your minds in Christ Jesus.

—Philippians 4:7 NIV

Thou will keep him in perfect peace, whose mind is stayed on thee: because he trusteth in thee.

—Isaiah 26:3 KJV

Peace I leave with you, my peace I give unto you, not as the world giveth, give I unto you. Let not your heart be troubled, neither let it be afraid.

—John 14:27 KJV

I will both lay me down in peace, and sleep: for thou, Lord, only makest me dwell in safety.

—Psalm 4:8 KJV

DAY ONE
Peace

Now may the Lord of peace himself give you peace at all times and in every way.

—2 Thessalonians 3:16 NIV

Jesus Christ is the Lord of peace. He wants you to have peace all the time, no matter the circumstances or situations in which you find yourself. But how can He give you peace if He does not know who you are?

Peace includes freedom from disturbance; a sense of being quiet and tranquil. Peace is also the awareness of the presence of God. The New Testament meaning of peace refers to rest and tranquility. When we are in the presence of God, our focus is on Him and not on our circumstances. Therefore, worry, fear, anxiety, and discouragement cannot exist while we are in God's presence. Isaiah 26:3 says it best: "Thou wilt keep him in perfect peace, whose mind is stayed on thee" (KJV). Peace is not the absence of trouble; it is the presence of God.

Peace comes in several forms: There is false peace, inner peace, peace with God, the peace of God, and peace with man (Romans 12:18 NKJV). We will discuss peace with God in the next segment. What is false peace? False peace is believing and acting as though all is well when all is *not* well: "They dress the wound of my people as though it were not serious. 'Peace, peace,' they say, when there is no peace" (Jeremiah 6:14 NIV).

Many of us experience false peace because of our desire to exercise our faith, calling those things that are not as though they are, often thinking we can overpower bad situations by overlooking them and proclaiming peace, yet we know all the time that peace is not in our hearts.

Inner peace refers to a state of being mentally and spiritually at peace, with enough knowledge and understanding to keep ourselves strong in the face of discord and stress (www.definitions.net). I like that definition, with enough knowledge and understanding (Colossians 1:9 KJV). According to Wikipedia, inner peace (peace of mind) refers to "a deliberate state of psychological or spiritual calm despite the potential presence of stressors." Inner peace relies on my ability to get enough of God's Word (knowledge) into my spirit and understand what it means for me.

One biblical commentary says that *peace* actually means "to tie together as a whole, when all essential parts are joined together." Inner peace, then, is wholeness of spirit and mind, a whole heart at rest. Inner peace often eludes us because we do not choose peace. We worry about our life situations, instead of getting in the presence of God.

Peace with men—what can be said about that? Romans 12:18 tells us, "If it is possible, as much as depends on you, live peaceably with all men" (NKJV; see also 2 Corinthians 13:11). We often find it difficult to live in peace with each other. I believe the reason for this has to do with our inability to resolve conflicts and an independent spirit (all about "what I want"). If we could only exercise the words of Jesus in Matthew 5:44: "But I say unto you, Love your enemies, bless them that curse you, do good to them that hate you, and pray for them which despitefully use you, and persecute you…" (KJV).

PRAYER

Father,

In the name of Jesus, I thank You for giving me peace. Thank You for being my peace. Thank You for Your peace that leads and guides me. Thank You for Your peace that keeps my heart and mind through Christ Jesus.

Thank You for delivering me from false peace. Thank You for my understanding of what false peace is and how to avoid walking in it.

I thank You for inner peace, which keeps my heart and mind at rest.

Most of all, I thank You for helping me to live at peace with other people. Yes, it is sometimes difficult, but my heart's desire is to be obedient to Your Word and "if at all possible, as much as lieth in me, live peaceable with all men" (Romans 12:18 NIV).

When that giant shows up, I thank You for the peace that passes all understanding, and the ability to quickly put my mind on You. Thank You for helping me to live in peace with all men.

I give You the glory and honor for who You are in my life. Amen.

REFLECTIONS

When was the last time you proclaimed peace when there was none? Explain your answer.

_____

_____

_____

_____

_____

_____

_____

_____

_____

_____

_____

_____

_____

_____

_____

_____

_____

_____

_____

_____

LIFE APPLICATION

How can you apply Matthew 5:44 to your life?

_____

_____

_____

_____

_____

_____

_____

_____

_____

_____

_____

_____

_____

_____

_____

_____

_____

_____

_____

_____

NOTES

Canaan City Limits: Roadblocks Ahead

DAY TWO
Peace with God

Therefore, being justified by faith, we have peace with God through our Lord Jesus Christ.

—Romans 5:1 KJV

Real lasting peace comes from having peace with God. This type of peace is the result of justification by faith. To be justified means to be declared righteous, and it only happens by faith. Justification is not a result of our works, but it comes only through faith in Christ and His finished work on the cross.

Justification makes it "just as if we had never sinned." We are not guilty—once and for all. Justification is therefore a state of acceptance by God. Why does man need this?

According to Isaiah 6:3, God is holy; man is not. God is light, and in Him is no darkness at all (1 John 1:5–6 KJV). God cannot accept evil, but we all have sinned (Romans 3:23 KJV). "When we were enemies, we were reconciled to God by the death of his Son..." (Romans 5:10 KJV).

We became enemies of God in the Garden of Eden. Adam and Eve deliberately disobeyed God. God had said to them, do not eat of the Tree of the Knowledge of Good and Evil, but they decided to do so anyway, and sin entered the world. Now man no longer has peace with God. Man can no longer fellowship with our Creator. We are now enemies of God. We need a Savior, a Deliverer, Someone who can make things right between man and God.

Jesus, the Prince of peace, gives us peace with God. He restored our relationship with God by dying on the cross and taking on the sins of the world: "The wages of sin is death; but the gift of God is eternal life through Jesus Christ our Lord" (Romans 6:23 KJV). We, as sinners, deserve death, and we are not able to pay the price for sin. Only a sinless Person, Jesus, was able to step up to the plate, and He did so, willing to become a sacrifice for the sins of the world.

"But he was pierced for our transgressions, he was crushed for our iniquities; the punishment that brought us peace was on him, and by his wounds we are healed" (Isaiah 53:5 NIV). He endured the beating so we could be free from the law of sin and death (Romans 8:2 KJV). We now can stand in God's presence. We now can live with Him for eternity.

Peace with God is conditional. Finding it is the first step toward having real peace in your life. Romans 10:9–10 is the means of receiving for yourself peace with God: "If you declare with your mouth, 'Jesus is Lord,' and believe in your heart that God raised him from the dead, you will be saved. For it is with your heart that you believe and are justified, and it is with your mouth that you profess your faith and are saved" (KJV). The word *if* at the beginning of this passage is a conditional word. You choose if you will or if you will not believe.

If you believe in your heart and confess with your mouth, it will put you in right standing with God. Put simply, peace with God is a restored relationship—reconciliation—between man and God. The moment we put our faith in Jesus, we are justified, and we become acceptable to God.

PRAYER

Father,

Thank You for making a way for me to be in fellowship with You, to commune with You, and to have an eternal relationship with You.

Thank You that I am no longer Your enemy.

Thank You that, from the very beginning of time, You knew people would need a Savior and that in time, Your Son, Jesus, would come to save the world.

Thank You that You sent someone to preach the Gospel to me, and that I heard the word and received it with gladness.

Thank You that lasting peace comes from having peace with You through my Lord, Jesus Christ.

In Jesus' name, I pray. Amen.

REFLECTIONS

When was the last time you deliberately disobeyed God? Explain your answer.

_____

_____

_____

_____

_____

_____

_____

Canaan City Limits: Roadblocks Ahead

LIFE APPLICATION

Do you have peace with God? Explain your answer.

_____

_____

_____

_____

_____

_____

_____

_____

_____

_____

_____

_____

_____

_____

_____

_____

_____

_____

_____

_____

NOTES

Canaan City Limits: Roadblocks Ahead

DAY THREE
Perfect Peace

You will keep him in perfect peace, whose mind is stayed on You, because he trusts in You.

—Isaiah 26:3 NKJV

Perfect peace comes from God, according to the above verse of Scripture. The word *perfect* has many connotations: "harmony," "wholeness," and "personal well-being," to name a few. Receiving perfect peace, however, has conditions that we must meet, conditions that require us to get involved in the process. So often we expect God to do all the work, but He has already done everything, objectively.

Now the subjective work of the Christian begins. Believers are not working to gain eternal life, but rather for the abundant life that is available here on earth. We are working to become more like Christ, which leads to the abundant life. What is this abundant life? And how do we live an abundant life? In Matthew 4:4, Jesus tells us, "It is written, 'Man shall not live by bread alone, but by every word that proceeds from the mouth of God" (NKJV). Could it be that the abundant life is based on how much of God's Word you know and apply? How much of God's Word you can speak into your life's situations? We should be living by whatever God has to say about what we are doing. Everything we say and do should be the result of what He has written, His Word, which has come out of His mouth.

Before we get into the conditions for perfect peace, let us first look at a few words from Isaiah 26:3 (NKJV): "You will keep him in perfect peace, whose mind is stayed on You, because he trusts in You."

- *Keep* means "to guard, protect, and maintain."
- *Mind* means our "imagination and thoughts."
- *Stayed* means "rooted and grounded, persuaded."
- *Trust* means "confident, sure, able to put confidence in."

Now, the first condition for receiving perfect peace is to keep your mind stayed on God, on the Lord Jesus Christ. The phrase "stayed on You" here refers to being rooted and grounded in God's Word. How do we keep our minds stayed on Him? More often than not, your mind easily wanders off, producing crazy thoughts and sometimes just going wild. In these times, we must take control of our minds and begin to think about God, meditate on Scripture, and refuse to give in to those thoughts that are not like God's. It is our responsibility to take control of our thoughts; asking God to control our thoughts is in vain.

Meditation is a key to keeping your mind stayed on Jesus. Practice thinking about God and Jesus. It is a choice that you alone can make. When you realize your mind is wandering and your thoughts are tending toward depression, you must counter them by speaking life over yourself: "I am fearfully and wonderfully made; God loves me, and I love Him; I am above and not beneath; God will never leave me nor forsake me!" As you speak life over yourself, you will find a new strength comes over you, a new excitement about life.

Think about the faithfulness of God. His promises are yes and amen ! Think on Christ and all He has done for you. Think about the cleansing power of the blood. "Set your mind on things above, not on things on the earth" (Colossians 3:2 NKJV). Be careful about what you allow to come into your mind (Proverbs 4:23 NKJV). Read the Bible regularly, for this is the only way to get the Word inside your heart and renew your mind. Doing all this and much, much more will keep you in perfect peace, and you will discover you trust Him with all that is within you.

> *Finally, brothers and sisters, whatever is true, whatever is noble, whatever is right, whatever is pure, whatever is lovely, whatever is admirable—if anything is excellent or praiseworthy—think about such things.*
> —Philippians 4:8 NIV

PRAYER

Father,

Thank You for perfect peace and the ability to experience it. Thank You for the provision You have made for me, and thank You for my responsibility to receive perfect peace from You. Thank You for the personal well-being that I experience and for the harmony in my life.

I will endeavor to keep my mind stayed on You, thinking about Jesus and meditating on Your Word.

I am persuaded of Your power and faithfulness; I am persuaded that Christ is Your Son and that He died so that I might have peace.

Thank You, Father, that I am rooted and grounded in Your Word, that Your Word is a lamp unto my feet and a light unto my path. Thank You for all these things, in Jesus' name. Amen.

REFLECTIONS

On what do you meditate the most? Be honest with yourself.

_____

_____

_____

_____

_____

_____

_____

_____

_____

_____

_____

_____

_____

_____

_____

_____

_____

LIFE APPLICATION

What will you start doing today in order to experience perfect peace?

_____

_____

_____

_____

_____

_____

_____

_____

_____

_____

_____

_____

_____

_____

_____

_____

_____

_____

NOTES

Canaan City Limits: Roadblocks Ahead

DAY FOUR
Life and Peace

For to be carnally minded is death; but to be spiritually minded is life and peace.

—Romans 8:6 KJV

The word *carnal* in the Greek means "flesh," "sensual," "meat of an animal," "the human body," and "human nature." *Carnal* covers a lot of territory, but to be carnally minded means that we gravitate to the human body or we give in to the desires of the body and trust in human nature more than we trust in God.

One of the most overused phrases today is this: "I'm only human." According to *Merriam-Webster*, the term *human nature* refers to characteristics of mankind. According to the *Free Dictionary*, the nature of humans consists of six characteristics, including being emotional, being rebellious, experiencing chaos, experiencing hard times, working for what we want, and having a self-image. These are qualities and ways of behaving that are natural and common to most people.

The carnal mind is not subject to the Law of God, meaning it refuses to take orders. The mind set on the flesh refuses to take orders from God's Word. The carnal mind is self-centered and hostile toward God. As a result, being carnally minded is death. "Death" here means deadly—it will kill (Romans 8:7–8 KJV).

Those who are in the flesh cannot please God. Why? Because nothing good is in the flesh: "For I know that in me (that is, in my flesh,) dwelleth no good thing" (Romans 7:18 KJV).

Carnal Christians live according to the dictates of the world, the flesh, and the devil. These are the three enemies of the believer, and we are charged to overcome them. First John 2:15 tells us, "Do not love the world or anything in the world. If anyone loves the world, love for the Father is not in them" (NKJV). Verse 16 goes on to say, "For everything in the world—the lust of the flesh, the lust of the eyes, and the pride of life—comes not from the Father but from the world." First Peter 5:8 also says, "Be alert and of sober mind. Your enemy the devil prowls around like a roaring lion looking for someone to devour" (NIV).

Carnality involves the desires of the flesh and physical relationships, while spirituality is concerned with the human spirit.

Carnal trust is toward the visible, while spirituality is concerned with trusting the invisible God.

The carnal man is controlled or dominated by the flesh or base appetites, while the spiritual man is dominated by a sense of oneness with God.

To be spiritually minded is life and peace. The word "life" is referring to *zoe*, the Greek word for the "God kind of life"—a life of abundance, which includes peace. This word *peace* means "quietness and rest." We all need this kind of peace. The carnal mind takes away this peace and replaces it with chaos. But oh, how we should thank God for the ability to develop a spiritual mind, which gives us life and peace. The key words in this section are:

- *Carnal:* flesh, the body, human nature
- *Death:* deadly
- *Life (zoe):* to live God's kind of life
- *Peace:* quietness, rest

PRAYER

Father,

In the name of Jesus, I thank You so much for Your Word. You sent Your Word to heal and deliver, and it always accomplishes its purpose.

Thank You for helping me to understand what it means to be carnal and what it means to be spiritual. Thank You that I do not have to live according to the flesh because You provided a way to overcome the flesh.

Walking in the Spirit, being led by You, Father, is the key to overcoming the carnal mind and its fleshly desires. A spiritual mind is life and peace, and I will endeavor to continually be renewed in my spirit so that I may experience life and peace according to Your Word.

In Jesus' name, amen.

REFLECTIONS

Are you clear on the meaning of a "carnal mind"? Explain what you believe it means.

_____

_____

_____

_____

Canaan City Limits: Roadblocks Ahead

LIFE APPLICATION

How do you deal with the three enemies of the believer?

_____

_____

_____

_____

_____

_____

_____

_____

_____

_____

_____

_____

_____

_____

_____

_____

_____

_____

_____

_____

_____

NOTES

Canaan City Limits: Roadblocks Ahead

SECTION 4
The Giant of Pride

- AMORITE: Giant of pride
- DEFINITION: Excessive self-esteem
- SOLUTION: Humility

MESSAGE TO THE OVERCOMER

"God resists the proud, but gives grace to the humble."
Therefore humble yourselves under the mighty hand of
God, that He may exalt you in due time.

—1 Peter 5:5–6 NKJV

Peter warns us from the beginning: "God resists the proud." This word *resists* comes from a Greek word meaning "to strive against, to oppose, and to stand firm against." Wow! Can you imagine what it would be like to have the almighty God opposing you, standing firm against you? Come to think of it, some of us may have experienced God in this way without even knowing what was going on.

Proud is the adjective form of the word *pride*. *Pride* refers to the pleasure that a person gets from something, such as their own achievements or skills. Saint Augustine defined *pride* as "the love of one's own excellence." Pride can be viewed as a positive or a negative characteristic. Too much pride results in a haughty spirit, which leads to behavior the Bible calls evil and a proud heart.

Feelings of pride produce a proud person. The adjective *proud* describes a person who acknowledges or expresses the pleasure received because of his accomplishments. Self-esteem is a form of pride, but excessive self-esteem is evil in God's sight. Excessive self-esteem produces a haughty spirit, a person who considers himself above his fellow man, preferring himself over others.

Luke 1:51 (NIV) provides an example of conceit (pride) in the heart that is never shown outwardly—but God knows each of our hearts. This reminds me of a recent incident in which my heart was exposed. I was parking my car (in a narrow space, I might add), and I scratched a parked car. I heard a noise, but I thought it was something on the ground. When I got out, I looked around but did not see anything. I never thought to look at the car next to me. I ran my errands, and when I got back to the car, two ladies were waiting on me. They showed me the front bumper of my car and how their paint was on it. We exchanged insurance information and identification and went our separate ways.

I tell this story because it revealed something in my inner-most heart I had no idea was there. God exposed to me the pride I had in never having had an accident or hit someone else's car. Now, I have never boasted outwardly about that, but somewhere deep inside I took pleasure in my "safe driver" status. The lesson learned was it is not about me or my ability; it is about the grace of God. Instead of feeling prideful, I should have been thanking God for keeping me safe and protecting me all these years.

Do not get me wrong. I have thanked God on many occasions for keeping a certain truck from hitting me or keeping a large piece of wood from coming through the windshield at a high rate of speed on the freeway. The bottom line to this story, though, is we should *always* remember to give God the glory, no matter the situation. Galatians 6:3 tells us, "If anyone thinks himself to be something, when he is nothing, he deceives himself" (NKJV).

Peter goes on to say that God gives grace to the humble. Grace is unearned favor, God giving us what we do not deserve. Grace is God's influence upon the heart. But this grace, this favor, is given to the humble. According to the dictionary, the word *humble* means "having or showing a modest or low estimate of one's own importance."

The word *meek* is a synonym for *humble*, and we know what the world says about the meek: It believes they are weak. The key phrase in this definition is a "modest estimate of one's own importance." This leads us to "humble yourselves under the mighty hand of God..." In addition, this is a command, not a suggestion. Humility does not come naturally to us; it must be "put on" (Colossians 3:12 NKJV). It must be added to our character by means of God's Spirit as we submit to Him. We either receive the benefits of humbling ourselves or the anguish that comes from being humbled by God.

Scripture is clear on this point concerning pride:

- Proverbs 16:18 (NKJV): "Pride goes before destruction."

- Proverbs 26:12 (NKJV): "Do you see a man wise in his own eyes? There is more hope for a fool than for him."
- Proverbs 15:25 (NKJV): "The LORD will destroy the house of the proud."
- Psalm 101:5 (NKJV): "The one who has a haughty look and a proud heart, him I will not endure."
- Daniel 4:37 (NKJV): Nebuchadnezzar declares, "Those who walk in pride He (God) is able to put down." (This was his experience.)

As we continue in Peter, we discover we can develop a low estimate of our own importance and allow God to exalt us in due time. When we obey Him and humble ourselves under the mighty hand of God, we reap the rewards of being exalted, which means "to be held in high regard," "to be raised to a higher rank or position."

What makes up a "mighty hand"? The word *mighty* translates to "powerful." God's mighty power is manifested in how He disciplines His children. Humility is a learned behavior, and God is the Master Teacher. When we refuse to humble ourselves under God's hand, what do you think happens?

Due time translates to "seasons," "an opportune time," or "an appropriate time." Oh my, this is an area that is difficult for us: waiting on God. We get so wrapped up in the right now, living in an instant-gratification world where waiting is not an option. Lord, help us, when time seems to go on and on without an answer, without a sign, without some direction from God, we start to falter. *How long must we wait?* we inwardly groan.

God's time is not our time. He sees time differently from us (2 Peter 3:8 NKJV).

A few characteristics of pride are found in Luke 18:9–14 (NKJV):

- A proud person cherishes independence, so that he will not be obligated to others.
- A proud person is preoccupied with self-proclaimed goodness; he never realizes he has any sin from which he needs to be saved.
- A proud person makes his own agenda without consideration of God or others; he considers his own best interest.
- A proud person tears others down to build up himself.
- A proud person shows a level of contempt for others.

MacLaren's Exposition calls humility "the slave's garment, a distinguishing mark of a slave." Humility is to know where my strength comes from and to not think more highly of myself than I ought to (Romans 12:3 NKJV). Humility is the preparation for service, and service is the test of humility. It is a different attitude entirely to serve others when you see yourself above them. Humility is the mark of a servant. Jesus took off His outer garments and tied a towel around His waist to wash His disciples' feet (John 13:4 NIV). So we should also take off the outer garment of our pride and tie on humility around our waist.

When you are living a life of humility and you come face-to-face with the giant of pride, it will not find anything in you with which it can identify. God's favor will usher you past that roadblock as you continue your journey to the Promised Land.

DAY ONE
Pride of Life

*For all that is in the world, the lust of the flesh, the lust
of the eyes, and the pride of life is not of the father but is
of the world.*

—1 John 2:16 NKJV

The *pride of life* is defined as anything that is of the world, self-confidence, comparison with others, and a pleasure with one's own life. An example in Scripture includes the story of the publican and the Pharisee praying in the temple (Luke 18:10–14 NKJV). The Pharisee prayed, "I am so glad I am not like that other person!" Pride is behavior that is based on envy. Adam Collier says, "The pride of life can look different for each person. To a businessperson it can be his title and his balance sheet; to the politician it can be his power and influence over others." J. Oswald Sanders, in his book *The Incomparable Christ*, describes the "pride of life" as an ambition to produce spiritual results by unspiritual means." Wow!

The pride of life will always be an issue in our lives, and overcoming it is a daily necessity. Just as the enemy tempted Jesus in the wilderness (Matthew 4:1–11 KJV), he is also tempting us, knowing that the pride of life will keep us out of the Promised Land. As long as we live in this world, we are encouraged to take pride in our education, take pride in how we look, and take pride in our accomplishments. We cannot escape it! We should follow Jesus' example. First, Jesus was well-versed in the Old Testament Scriptures (the only source of God's Word at that time in history). He was able to counter the enemy with the Word of God. And not only did He counter it, but He was specific with His choice of the Scripture verses that He used.

Jesus was fasting in the wilderness when the enemy showed up and told Him to turn the rocks to bread. Jesus countered, "Man shall not live by bread alone, but by every word that proceeds out of the mouth of God." That is a specific Scripture that He used to address and counteract the temptation. Is it any wonder why we need to know what God has to say to us in the Bible? The Bible addresses every issue of life, and we should want to search the Scriptures to find the answers we need.

PRAYER

Father,

In the name of Jesus, thank You for Your goodness, kindness, mercy, joy, and love. Thank You for showing us how to live.

You sent Your Word to heal and to deliver, and I am grateful that Your Word is available to me. Thank You for the ability to read Your Word, to memorize Your Word, to speak forth Your Word, and to share Your Word with others. Life is found in Your Word, and I desire to have life more abundantly.

Father, thank You for walking with me, talking with me, and leading me in paths of righteousness for Your name's sake. I know it is possible to overcome that giant called the pride of life if I continue to read and

trust Your Word.
   In the name of Jesus, I pray. Amen.

REFLECTIONS

How do you define your personal pride of life? Be specific.

_____

_____

_____

_____

_____

_____

_____

_____

_____

_____

_____

_____

_____

_____

_____

_____

_____

_____

_____

LIFE APPLICATION

With what temptation do you struggle the most? What Scriptures do you use to overcome it?

_____

_____

_____

_____

_____

_____

_____

_____

_____

_____

_____

_____

_____

_____

_____

_____

_____

_____

NOTES

DAY TWO
Pride Brings Low

A man's pride will bring him low, but the humble in spirit will retain honor.

—Proverbs 29:23 NKJV

It takes no stretch of the imagination to understand what it means to "bring someone low." In today's society, we are drawn to stare at the downfalls of the rich and famous. We are aware of their issues through social media and "instant news." However, there is a group whose pride might not get instant exposure to the world. That group includes the normal everyday people in our society.

As a rule, prideful people are not well-received. We tend to step back from those who are selfish, those who only exalt their needs and desires. Pride always points to self, which is a natural human tendency. Again, choice is the hallmark of the humble person, one who chooses others rather than self: "What doth the LORD require of thee, but to do justly, and to love mercy, and to walk humbly with thy God?" (Micah 6:8 KJV).

I like what Proverbs 15:33 says: "Before honor is humility" (NKJV). Another word for "honor" in the Hebrew is "glory." Can you think of a person who humbled himself only to be exalted later?

A preacher friend went to a church event and decided to sit in the back of the church and not be seen. As he became comfortable in the back, the pastor of the church sent for him to come up front. When he humbled himself, God exalted him to a place of honor. I also heard the story of a young preacher who attended a church event and decided to go sit in the pulpit. A little bit later, a more renowned minister arrived and was escorted to the front and the younger preacher was asked to give up his seat in what became an awkward situation (Proverbs 25:6–7 NKJV).

The Bible contains many examples of people with haughty hearts and how God resisted them. One of the first examples is Lucifer. Isaiah 14:12–14 (NKJV) shares the account of Lucifer, the son of the morning. Pride filled his heart, and soon he began to plan to ascend into the heavens and exalt himself above God. His desire was to be like the Most High. It is bad enough to lift yourself above your fellow man, but when you think you know better than even God, trouble is on the horizon. Lucifer, the morning star, was tossed out of heaven, and his name was changed to Satan, which means "adversary."

Lucifer was incredibly beautiful. Ezekiel 28:12 (NKJV) describes him as the "seal of perfection, full of wisdom and perfect in beauty." Verse 15 says, "You were perfect in your ways from the day you were created, till iniquity was found in you." The word *iniquity* comes from the Hebrew word meaning "evil." That evil, proud heart led to his downfall. He chose to rebel against God because of his beauty (Proverbs 16:18 NKJV).

Another example of pride is found in the life of King Nebuchadnezzar. Daniel 4:30–32 (NKJV) tells us how God humbled this king: "The king spoke, saying, 'Is not this great Babylon, that I have built for a royal dwelling by my mighty power and for the honor of my majesty?' While the word was still in the king's mouth, a voice fell from heaven: 'King Nebuchadnezzar, to you it is spoken: the kingdom has departed from you! And they shall drive you from men, and your dwelling shall be with the beasts of the field. They shall make you eat grass like oxen; and seven times shall pass over you, until you know that the Most High rules in the kingdom of men, and gives it to whomever He chooses.'" In Luke 14:11 (NKJV), Jesus said, "For whoever exalts himself will be humbled, and he who humbles himself will be exalted."

Pride sets God against us, because we have the nerve to think we are greater than God or that we have what we own by our own power. In short, that is an attempt to steal God's glory, and He will not have it: "And at the end of the time I, Nebuchadnezzar, lifted my eyes to heaven, and my understanding returned to me; and I blessed the Most High and praised and honored Him who lives forever" (Daniel 4:34 NKJV).

Pride impacts us all. But the humble in spirit will overcome the giant of pride and maintain their honor while on the way to the Promised Land.

PRAYER

Father,

Thank You for Your Word, which You sent to heal and to deliver me. Thank You for Your Word in Romans 15:4: "For everything that was written in the past was written to teach us, so that through the endurance taught in the Scriptures and the encouragement they provide we might have hope" (niv). Thank You for the ability to learn from King Nebuchadnezzar and from the fallen angel Lucifer. God, You are all-powerful, and nothing happens without Your knowledge.

Father, thank You for the warnings You give in Your Word about pride and how we should learn to humble ourselves so that You will not need to do it for us. In Jesus' name, amen.

REFLECTIONS

Name an incident when pride was a problem for you. Explain.

_____

_____

_____

_____

_____

_____

_____

_____

_____

_____

_____

_____

_____

_____

_____

_____

_____

_____

LIFE APPLICATION

In what areas of your life do you need to be humbler in spirit? Explain.

_____

_____

_____

_____

_____

_____

_____

_____

_____

_____

_____

_____

_____

_____

_____

_____

_____

NOTES

_____

_____

_____

_____

_____

_____

_____

_____

_____

_____

_____

_____

_____

_____

_____

_____

_____

_____

_____

_____

_____

_____

_____

_____

_____

DAY THREE
God Gives Grace

*But he giveth more grace. Wherefore he saith, God
resisteth the proud, but giveth grace unto the humble.*

—James 4:6 KJV

Grace is usually defined as "God's unmerited favor toward
man." Grace is God not giving us what we deserved,
which is judgment and death. Grace is God's ability made
available to us, so that when I am weak, then God can be
strong in my life (2 Corinthians 12:9 KJV).

The humble person has a sense of their own weakness
and depravity and puts no confidence in anything they are or
anything they have. The humble see their need for grace, i.e.,
their need for God. Humility is a key attribute for receiving
salvation, the gift of God: "For by grace you have been saved
through faith, and that not of yourselves; it is the gift of God"
(Ephesians 2:8 NKJV).

The humble can accept their need for a Savior. They accept
their sinful state and believe on Jesus, who died for them,
thereby receiving grace, favor, and the power to enter God's
presence and become part of His family. That is grace: God
giving us what we do not deserve.

In contrast, the proud resist the notion of needing anyone
besides themselves. The proud put their confidence in their
own abilities and power and seek the praise of men rather than

the praise of God. They resist the truth of God in their under-standing, and in their will, they resist the laws of God. The proud have a high and unreasonable estimation of their own excellence and importance.

Matthew Henry's commentary suggests that we should submit our understanding to the truth of God; submit our will to the will of God's precepts, the will of his providence; and submit ourselves to God, for He is ready to do us good.

To *submit* means "to accept or yield to a superior force, or to the authority or will of another person." Submission is the action of accepting or yielding to a superior force or to the will or authority of another person. Submitting means putting others before yourself, not always doing what you want to do. Submission to God means putting His desires above your own. This also moves us into the area of obeying laws and those in authority: "Let every soul be subject unto the higher powers. For there is no power but of God: the powers that be are ordained of God" (Romans 13:1 KJV).

Oh, how we resist authority, because we want what we want! We want to do our own thing, which leads to a haughty and proud spirit. God resists the proud, but He gives grace to the humble. When we purpose in our heart to submit to Him and humble ourselves, God pours upon us the ability and the power to walk humbly before Him. He gives more grace to the humble in spirit. Certainly it takes more of God's ability to overcome the giant of pride that blocks our entrance into the Promised Land.

PRAYER

Father,

In the name of Jesus, I thank You for Your grace working in my life. Thank You that Your grace gives me the ability to handle any situation in life through Your strength. Thank You for the humility to receive Your grace.

I know that of myself I can do nothing, but with Your help, Your power, and Your willingness, I can do all things. Your grace makes it possible. I pray that I will walk humbly before You and receive more grace in this life.

In Jesus' name, amen.

REFLECTIONS

Name a time when you felt like you did not need anyone besides yourself. Explain.

_____

_____

_____

_____

_____

_____

_____

_____

_____

_____

Canaan City Limits: Roadblocks Ahead

LIFE APPLICATION

In what areas of your life do you need to submit more to God? Explain.

_____

_____

_____

_____

_____

_____

_____

_____

_____

_____

_____

_____

_____

_____

_____

_____

_____

NOTES

DAY FOUR
Before Honor

*Before destruction the heart of a man is haughty, and
before honor is humility.*

—Proverbs 18:12 NKJV

Proverbs, the book of wisdom, has much to say about how to
live, and for this writing, much about pride and humility.
Proverbs 15:33 states, "The fear of the LORD is the instruction
of wisdom, and before honor is humility" (NKJV). Humility is
a choice that we daily strive to make, but we never fully arrive.
Each day brings new situations in which we must choose
humility. Humility is a command (1 Peter 5:6 KJV). How can
we be gentle, patient, submissive, and long-suffering toward
others without humility? I do not think we can, because they
require us to be selfless, not to think highly of ourselves, and to
love our neighbor as ourselves.

Rachel Brunner from Learn Religion says this:

> *Humility makes us more childlike; it makes us teachable.*
> *Humility is required for forgiveness, the forgiveness
> of our sins.*
> *Weakness becomes our strength; it helps us to be
> humble.*

For I say, through the grace given to me, to everyone who is among you, not to think of himself more highly than he ought to think, but to think soberly, as God has dealt to each one a measure of faith.

—Romans 12:3 NKJV

Humility prepares people for honor. Honor means "esteem" or "great respect," "to value someone highly." Honor is the reward of humility. Honor is an internal attitude, but it should have appropriate outward action. God honors us by letting others see how He values us. We should reciprocate by showing others that we honor God in every area of our lives (John 12:26 KJV), and that we value Him. Honor is a reward for righteous living, humility, and faithfulness to God (Proverbs 21:21 NKJV).

Just a few comments about destruction and haughtiness: "Before destruction, the heart of a man is haughty" (Proverbs 18:12 KJV). This entire section has been about pride and how to overcome that old giant. A haughty heart is a proud heart, vain and arrogant. This kind of heart only thinks of self; it is egotistical and condescending. Is it any wonder that destruction is the result of such a heart? Some other meanings for *destruction* are "demolition," "eradication," and "killing." A haughty heart is on the same path as the enemy: to steal, kill, and destroy. And in this instance, it brings self-destruction.

Finally, Proverbs 22:4 states: "Humility is the fear of the Lord; its wages are riches and honor and life" (NIV).

ADDITIONAL READING

- Romans 12:10 NIV
- Proverbs 27:18 NIV

PRAYER

Father,

Thank You for Your instruction to humble myself. Humility is so important to my relationship with You. Thank You that I am important to You, and that You want to use me to bless Your people. If I continue to think more highly of myself than I should, then I am not in a good position to be used by You.

Father, Your honor of me is much better than me lifting my own self up. Thank You for teaching me how to walk humbly with You. Thank You for the ability to think more highly of others. "Humility is the fear of the Lord; its wages are riches and honor and life," according to Proverbs 22:4 (NIV).

In Jesus' name, amen.

REFLECTIONS

What is your understanding of the phrase "humility comes before honor"?

_____

_____

_____

_____

Canaan City Limits: Roadblocks Ahead

LIFE APPLICATION

Compare Proverbs 25:27 with Proverbs 27:2. How do these verses fit into your life?

_____

_____

_____

_____

_____

_____

_____

_____

_____

_____

_____

_____

_____

_____

_____

_____

_____

_____

_____

NOTES

SECTION 5
The Giant of Lack of Discipline

- PERIZZITE: Unwalled
- DEFINITION: Lack of self-control, lack of discipline
- SOLUTION: The fruit of the Spirit (Galatians 5:22–23 KJV)

MESSAGE TO THE OVERCOMER

And those who are Christ's have crucified the flesh with its passions and desires.

—Galatians 5:24 NKJV

Whenever the word *crucified* comes up, we immediately think of the cross of Christ. The word *crucified* comes from the Greek root word meaning "self-denial." Mark 8:34 (NKJV) gives us these words of Jesus: "Whoever desires to come after Me, let him deny himself, and take up his cross, and follow me." This leads us to the meaning of self. Self is the fleshly, carnal life of nature, the life of the first Adam, "dead in trespasses and sins" (Ephesians 2:1 KJV), thoroughly corrupt before God (Galatians 5:19–21 KJV), living a life in which there is no good thing in the sight of God (Romans 7:18 KJV).

Self-denial denotes the action an individual must take. No one can make the decision for you. It is your choice and yours alone. Thus, the same is true for self-control. Self must decide to take control over its desires and passions, denying our human nature and its impulses for self-gratification. Self-discipline is willing yourself to do what is right despite your feelings. Self-discipline, self-denial, and self-control all boil down to possessing power and mastery over oneself, over our own human nature.

According to Jon Bloom, "The secret to self-discipline lies in the prize. What are we willing to endure self-denial to have? The power of self-discipline comes from the prize we want— the reward we believe will yield us the greatest pleasure." That is so true. Think about it in your own life. I often tell people that once we make up our minds about a thing, we will put every effort into accomplishing it. The pleasure of the prize must outweigh the pleasure of self-indulgence.

Self-control is a goal, meaning we do not sin because of ignorance, but we sin because we simply will not make the sacrifice to control ourselves. "Self-control is not a lack of willpower but of award power," writes Jon Bloom.

He who is slow to anger is better than the mighty. And he who rules his spirit than he who takes a city.
—Proverbs 16:32 NIV

He who is slow to wrath has great understanding, but he who is impulsive exalts folly.

—Proverbs 14:29 NIV

First Corinthians 9:24–27 (NIV) speaks of running a race, and the purpose is to receive the prize. The apostle Paul then encourages us to "run in such a way that you may obtain it" (verse 24). In the natural, we understand the training that must take place for any athlete to become the best and win the prize. Verse 25 of this chapter declares: "And everyone who competes for the prize is temperate in all things" (NKJV).

The word *temperate* means to "show moderation or self-restraint." Again, we see the word *self* here. Self must restrain the desires and passions that lead to a lack of temperance. When an athlete loses motivation or is not on top of his or her game, the coach or trainer encourages the athlete to keep their eyes on the prize. Remember, the power in self-discipline comes from the prize that gives greater pleasure than the sacrifice.

Okay, gold medal winners, club champions, most valuable players, you gave up much to reach your goal. You ran the race; you were temperate; you exercised self-denial and gave up immediate gratification in order to win the prize.

Overcomers, the solution to being unwalled, out of control, and undisciplined is the fruit of the Spirit (Galatians 5:22–23 NIV). By ourselves, we have no self-control, but temperance is a fruit of the Spirit. If the Spirit of Christ dwells in you, then you can draw on His power to help you exercise discipline in your life. Listen for the still, small voice within to lead you and guide you into all truth.

Listed below are a few ways to strengthen your spirit and your resolve to overcome the unwalled, undisciplined giant:

- *Prayer:* 1 Thessalonians 5:17 (NIV)
- *Worship*: Hebrews 12:28 (NIV)
- *Fasting*: Joel 2:12 (NIV)
- *Confession of sin*: Proverbs 28:13 (NIV); 1 John 1:9 (NIV)
- *Bible study*: "When you spend time in the mind of God, your mind will become like the mind of God," Pastor Tom Hendrikse has said.

DAY ONE
Control Your Spirit

Whoever has no rule over his own spirit is like a city broken down, without walls.

—Proverbs 25:28 NKJV

The Amplified Bible adds more details to this verse: "Like a city that is broken down and without walls (leaving it unprotected) is a man who has no self-control over his spirit [and sets himself up for trouble]."

Ellicott's Commentary on the phrase "Like a city broken down, without walls" indicates that the city is now exposed to the assault of every temptation. There are no restraints on his passions, desires, and affections.

Can you imagine being that out of control, so much that there are no restraints on your behavior? I do not know the ins and outs of the mentality of a serial killer, a serial rapist, a serial womanizer, or a serial abuser, but "serial" means they repeatedly commit the same offense; they follow a certain behavior pattern.

I chose this list of serial behavior because it is shocking, and we hear about this type of behavior because of the lawlessness of it. But think about the legitimate desires and passions that are out of control in your own life! Any and everything is up for grabs. Imagine there is no monitor or internal voice telling you, "Stop, that is enough." Or perhaps you simply ignore that voice because your desire is stronger than the voice.

How does a person rule over his own spirit? The word *rule* means "to regulate, oversee, make decisions for, and reign over." The spirit is the inner man of the heart, having the ability to think, to will, and to experience strong emotions. Ruling over the spirit means to regulate your will, to take charge of what you think about, and to reign over your emotions. The word *reign* denotes sovereign power. Maintain power and control over how you live, and exercise temperance in all that you do.

A life without walls, without barriers, without boundaries, or without protection is full of trouble. This type of life extends itself over others' lives, as if your desires and wants are more important than anyone else's. Self-control is the power to rule over all your affections and passions.

Self-control is a fruit of the Spirit, which is the power of God. What help do we have to control our spirits?

- The Holy Spirit
- The sense of the presence of Christ, the knowledge that a holy God is watching you and walking with you
- Charity in the heart: A loving person is not worried by envies or enmities

Conquering yourself is difficult. It is challenging to fight against our sin nature, and that lets us know we need help. Psalm 31:5 says, "Into your hands I commit my spirit; deliver me, Lord, my faithful God" (NIV). We know of the struggles of David, but we also know he was a man after God's own heart (Acts 13:22 NIV). David was not perfect, but he responded properly when he was confronted with his sin. We, too, should learn how to run to God in our most difficult times (Psalm 69:17 NIV).

As you draw near to your Promised Land, be prepared to overcome that "no self-control" roadblock with a life that is pleasing to God.

PRAYER

Father,

In the name of Jesus, I do not want to be like a city broken down and without walls. Thank You for teaching me how to bring my body under subjection. Though I struggle, my desire is to regulate my will to Your praise and glory.

Thank You, Father, for I now understand my lack of control affects all those around me. I desire to be a witness to Your power in my life. Thank You for continuing to work within me both the will and the action to do Your good pleasure. Thank You for the ability to restrain my behavior.

In Jesus' name, amen.

REFLECTIONS

What are your thoughts about those who repeatedly commit the same offense (as in the meaning of the word *serial*)?

_____

_____

_____

_____

_____

_____

_____

_____

_____

_____

_____

_____

_____

_____

_____

_____

_____

_____

_____

_____

LIFE APPLICATION

What legitimate desires and passions are out of control in your life? Be honest with yourself.

_____

_____

_____

_____

_____

_____

_____

_____

_____

_____

_____

_____

_____

_____

_____

_____

_____

_____

_____

NOTES

DAY TWO
Control Your Body

It is God's will that you should be sanctified: that you should avoid sexual immorality; that each of you should learn to control your own body in a way that is holy and honorable, not in passionate lust like the pagans, who do not know God.

—1 Thessalonians 4:3–5 NIV

On day one of this section, we discussed controlling the spirit. Now we are focusing in on controlling the body. What is the difference between the body and the spirit? The answer should be obvious but let's take a look (1 Thessalonians 5:23 NIV).

The human spirit is the part of us that can know God intimately. Our relationship to God is spirit to Spirit. When His Spirit lives in the believer, only then can we commune with Him (John 4:24 NIV). Our human spirit then connects with God, and to be connected with God is to be alive spiritually. Ephesians 2:4–5 tells us, "God… made us alive with Christ even when we were dead in transgressions—it is by grace you have been saved" (NIV). John 5:24 says that we have "crossed over from death to life" (NIV). It is not a physical death, but we move from spiritual death into a spiritual life.

The physical body is the part of the person in which both soul and spirit are contained. "God created man from the dust of the ground" (Genesis 2:7 KJV), resulting in having a physical body. The body connects with its surroundings, as seen in Genesis 2:19–20. The body is world-conscious; the soul is self-conscious; and the spirit is God-conscious.

The body is like a servant, under man's control. Either the soul is giving directions, or the spirit of man is giving directions. The body yields to the strongest ruler. The soul rules over the body until it yields its power and authority to the spirit. The body responds to whichever is in control and giving it orders. The soul of man communicates with the physical world through the body, and the spirit of man communicates with the spiritual realm through the spirit. To paraphrase a comment from Watchman Nee, the soul determines if the spirit realm is to rule or if the physical realm is to rule.

Romans 12:2 (NIV) reminds us not to be controlled by the world. The body identifies and communicates with the world. Is it any wonder why it is so important to control the body? First Thessalonians 4:4 tells us to "learn to control your own body" (NIV). The learning starts with understanding the difference between soul and spirit. Soul relates to the natural life and is all about itself. So, "self" can easily move the body into various activities. When the soul motivates the body, it is all about self-gratification.

God desires the body to be holy and honorable. When the spirit of man is in charge, the body will glorify God, thus teaching us how to control our own body. In 1 Corinthians 9:27 (KJV), Paul says he brings his body into subjection. That word *subjection* comes from a Greek word that means "to enslave." Paul did not allow his body to do whatever it wanted to do. His body was a slave to Paul's spirit, with no rights of its own. When the soul controls the body, it will lead to the fulfillment of passionate lusts; when the spirit controls the body, it honors God. The soul is flesh. Galatians 5:19–21 (KJV) speaks of the works of the flesh; Galatians 5:22–23 (KJV) speaks of the fruit of the Spirit.

PRAYER

Father,

In the name of Jesus, thank You for showing me how the spirit, soul, and body communicate with one another. Thank You for helping me understand how to control my own body. Thank You for the ability to choose to walk in the Spirit, thereby honoring You. Thank You, Father, for teaching me the difference between my soul and my spirit. Thank You that my relationship with You is based on my spirit and not my flesh.

I can only worship You in spirit, and I desire to have a relationship with You, my heavenly Father. That can only happen as I live life in the Spirit. Thank You, Father.

In Jesus' name, amen.

REFLECTIONS

How does the fruit of the Spirit fit into how you can take control of your body?

_____

_____

_____

_____

_____

_____

_____

_____

_____

_____

_____

_____

_____

_____

_____

_____

_____

_____

_____

_____

_____

LIFE APPLICATION

Are you alive spiritually? How do you know?

_____

_____

_____

_____

_____

_____

_____

_____

_____

_____

_____

_____

_____

_____

_____

_____

_____

_____

_____

_____

_____

_____

NOTES

DAY THREE
Exercise Self-Control

*And everyone who competes for the prize is temperate in
all things. Now they do it to obtain a perishable crown,
but we for an imperishable crown.*

—1 Corinthians 9:25 NKJV

Previously we discussed controlling your spirit and controlling your own body. It may seem like I have put the cart before the horse in that self-control is the beginning, the major factor when control is an issue. However, these first two topics show the importance of the need for self-control.

Some areas in need of self-control are:

- Temptations: Avoid temptations that can draw you away from God.
- Bad company: "Bad company corrupts good character" (1 Corinthians 15:33 NIV); "Do not be deceived" (Galatians 6:7 NIV).
- Evil: "Abstain from every form of evil" (1 Thessalonians 5:22 NIV); reject every kind of evil.

It is impossible to avoid exposure to everything that is sinful; thus, exercising self-control is paramount. You are in control when you "set your mind on things above" (Colossians 3:2 NIV), when you think on these things: "whatever things are true, whatever things are noble, whatever things are just, whatever things are pure, whatever things are lovely, whatever things are of good report, if there is any virtue and if there is anything praiseworthy—meditate on these things" (Philippians 4:8 NKJV).

Become a slave to righteousness, not to sin (Romans 6:16–18 NKJV). Make a conscious decision to focus on God rather than on temptation. We are not tempted by the things we hate: "Abhor what is evil. Cling to what is good" (Romans 12:9 NKJV).

Self-control is about controlling *you*. You are practicing self-control when you make yourself do the right thing. Self-control is not about others keeping you from doing something. Yet, we often find ourselves asking God to keep us from sinning, keep us from cursing, from fighting, from committing adultery, and the list goes on. The Holy Spirit gives us the power to have self-control, but we must choose to use it. When the Spirit speaks, we should listen and obey.

Self-control closes the list of the fruit of the Spirit just as drunkenness and reviling closes the list of the works of the flesh. Self-control is not gained by suppressing, but by controlling the lusts of the flesh. What is the difference?

To *suppress* means "to put an end to, especially with force; to crush, to do away with, to prohibit and subdue."

To *control* is "to exercise influence over, to suggest or dictate the behavior of others." *Control* is "influence over or authority over others."

Willpower is at the forefront of suppression. Willpower (the power of the will) can temporarily suppress your urges. However, suppressing urges does not make them magically disappear; they still will continue to grow until you are no longer able to ignore them.

Again, self-control is the ability to regulate one's emotions, thoughts, and behavior in the face of temptations and impulses. According to an internet article, "Three Types of Self-Control," by the Understood Team, "There is impulse control, emotional control, and movement control. Impulse control is the ability to stop and think before acting. It lets us think through consequences before we do something. Emotional control is the ability to manage feelings. It helps us keep going, even when upsetting or unexpected things happen. Movement control is the ability to control how our body moves. It lets us regulate what we do physically in an appropriate way."

As you can see, self-control is important to the Christian life. That is why we need the Holy Spirit to lead us in this area of controlling the self (the flesh). The flesh has no desire to be under control. Instant gratification is all it wants. But thanks be to God, we have the victory over the flesh.

PRAYER

Father,

How I long to control my natural impulses. Self-control is not what the flesh desires. My desire is to be like Christ, to walk in the Spirit and not fulfill the lust of the flesh.

Thank You for showing me that suppressing or holding back my unhealthy desires is not the answer. Thank You for Your Word, which shows me how to take control over my mind, over temptations, over bad company, and over evil. I realize I am in control when I think on things that are good and pure, and when I set my mind on things above. Thank You for showing me

that willpower can never take the place of self-control.
In Jesus' name, amen.

REFLECTIONS

What is the difference between willpower and self-control?

_____

_____

_____

_____

_____

_____

_____

_____

_____

_____

_____

_____

_____

_____

_____

_____

_____

_____

_____

_____

LIFE APPLICATION

In which areas of your life do you suppress temptations and desires?

_____

_____

_____

_____

_____

_____

_____

_____

_____

_____

_____

_____

_____

_____

_____

_____

_____

_____

_____

_____

NOTES

DAY FOUR
Temperance

And beside this, giving all diligence, add to your faith virtue; and to virtue knowledge; and to knowledge temperance; and to temperance patience; and to patience godliness; and to godliness brotherly kindness; and to brotherly kindness charity.

—2 Peter 1:5–7 KJV

The above verse of Scripture describes the process of Christian growth. The key words here are "add to," and it all starts with faith. The main ingredient, the foundation, the beginning of the Christian life is *faith.* Faith puts us on the road to growth, and as our faith grows, we then can add virtue or character. This Scripture leads me to believe that if faith is the foundation, and everything after that is added, then first things first come into play. For instance, you cannot add virtue to faith if you do not first have faith.

This portion of our study will focus on temperance, which is added to knowledge. Why do you think temperance follows the gaining of knowledge? *Knowledge* is defined as "the facts, information, and skills acquired by a person through experience or education; the theoretical or practical understanding of a subject." Also, knowledge is "an awareness or familiarity gained by experience of a fact or situation." Knowledge is an understanding of what God would have us to do. Knowledge comes from God and His Word. God is the Source of true knowledge, and His Word teaches us what God expects from us as Christians, as His children.

> *The fear of the LORD is the beginning of knowledge.*
> —Proverbs 1:7 kjv

Your reverence for and your obedience to God is the beginning of knowledge. Hosea 4:6–7 (kjv) tells us that lack of knowledge will destroy a people.

Without knowledge and understanding, temperance will not have a foundation on which to stand. How would we know what our parameters are? How would we know there is even such a thing as temperance? How would we know that God wants us to live above our animal, fleshly tendencies, to live a life based on the truth of His Word, to know, believe, and heed (put into action)?

Temperance is the ability to control appetites, emotions, and attitudes. It is the ability to resist sin. One writer says, "It is the ability to turn down opportunities for the excess of good things." Temperance helps us control our physical desire for pleasure. Gluttony is the lack of temperance regarding food; drunkenness is the lack of temperance regarding alcoholic beverages.

Incontinence, another word related to *temperance*, is "the inability to control one's appetites, emotions, and attitudes; lacking self-restraint; uncontrolled." Our culture uses the word *incontinent* to politely describe those who have lost the ability to hold their bladder, those who have no or insufficient voluntary control. Incontinence is messy, embarrassing, and inconvenient. Did you know that the word *incontinent* is in the Bible? Second Timothy 3:2–3 states, "For men shall be lovers of their own selves, covetous, boasters, proud, blasphemers, disobedient to parents, unthankful, unholy, without natural affection, trucebreakers, false accusers, incontinent, fierce, despisers of those that are good" (KJV).

Temperance should be a priority in the life of a Christian. Imagine what life could be if you had the power of God to do what you know you should do all the time. Temperance is a characteristic of Christian leadership (Titus 1:8 KJV). Temperance is necessary for Christian growth, for it gives you the power to resist temptation (2 Peter 1:6 KJV). Temperance is needed to successfully follow Christ. Your flesh will lead you away from Jesus (Matthew 16:24 KJV).

How can we obtain temperance? It begins with a decision, the choice to live a holy life. In Daniel 1:8 (NIV), Daniel purposed in his heart that he would not defile himself. God's Word tells us to be filled with the Spirit (Ephesians 5:18 KJV; Galatians 5:22–23 KJV). Temperance is not a learned skill; it is a product of the Spirit-filled life. In Job 31:1, Job himself said, "I made a covenant with mine eyes; why then should I think upon a maid?" (KJV). Do you remember Achan, in Joshua 7:21, and his lack of temperance? He said, "I coveted them and took them" (NKJV). This caused him and his entire family to be executed by stoning, the dire consequences for their disobedience. The lack of temperance is serious and leads to destruction.

PRAYER

Write out your prayer here.

_____

_____

_____

_____

_____

_____

_____

_____

_____

_____

_____

_____

_____

_____

_____

_____

_____

_____

_____

_____

_____

_____

REFLECTIONS

How do self-control and temperance relate to each other?

_____

_____

_____

_____

_____

_____

_____

_____

_____

_____

_____

_____

_____

_____

_____

_____

_____

_____

_____

_____

_____

_____

LIFE APPLICATION

Is a lack of temperance affecting your life? In what area(s)?
How?

_____

_____

_____

_____

_____

_____

_____

_____

_____

_____

_____

_____

_____

_____

_____

_____

_____

_____

_____

_____

NOTES

_____

_____

_____

_____

_____

_____

_____

_____

_____

_____

_____

_____

_____

_____

_____

_____

_____

_____

_____

_____

_____

_____

SECTION 6
The Giant of Depression

- CANAANITES: Depression
- DEFINITION: Hopelessness, being below the standard, sadness
- SOLUTION: Hope

MESSAGE TO THE OVERCOMER

Men ought always to pray, and not to faint.

—Luke 18:1 KJV

There are three million cases of depression per year in the United States; it is said to be more common in females, and the most common age of those who suffer from depression is between fifteen and forty-five years old. According to *Time* magazine, September 05, 2020, issue, "Depression has skyrocketed during the Covid-19 pandemic, almost as soon as the lockdown went into effect." *Psychology Today* reports that the "Covid-19 pandemic has increased loneliness in Americans, and that loneliness is associated with rates of depression and suicidal ideation."

Clinical depression, as it is called, involves more than just having the blues; it is a serious mood disorder. It is not known, definitively, what causes depression, but its symptoms are identifiable. Some of these symptoms include feeling sad, feeling empty, tearfulness, irritability, frustration, loss of interest, lack of energy, feelings of worthlessness, unexplained physical problems, angry outbursts, thoughts of death, and suicide attempts. What a list!

Depression as a noun is "the state of feeling sad, melancholy, a mood disorder." *Depressed* as an adjective describes a person who is in a state of general unhappiness or despondency.

Because depression has no definitive root cause, only its symptoms are treated. This has led to the idea that depression does not have a cure, and we can only find temporary relief from its symptoms. The relief usually comes through the use of antidepressant medication and psychotherapy, the world's solution to what it calls a "serious mental health condition."

As a young adult, I often had bouts of melancholy. I wanted to die, but I could not commit suicide because of something I heard at some point in my growing-up days: "God will not forgive you if you commit suicide." That idea helped me to live a miserable life for years. *Melancholy* is a "feeling of sadness, typically with no obvious cause; a gloomy state of mind, wrapped up in sorrowful thoughts." The key phrase here is "wrapped up in sorrowful thoughts." If you look at the other symptoms of depression, *self* is clearly at the center, the core of the problem.

For me, I was sick of life. There was nothing that brought pleasure to my life. Short of suicide, my only option was to find ways to dull my thoughts and feelings. I am sure it is similar with medical treatment; however, traditional medicine was not my choice for relieving the pain of sadness and emptiness, nor my thoughts of feeling all alone in the world, that nobody cared about me. Medicine and therapy can be effective ways to treat depression. Therapy teaches people how to cope with conflicts and traumas, while antidepressants only reduce symptoms. This leads us to the biblical solutions for depression, and how they saved me from a life of despair.

Psalm 42:5 (NASB1995) says it all: "Why are you in despair, O my soul? And why have you become disturbed within me?" *Despair* means "the complete loss or absence of hope." *Disturbed* means "to be agitated or distressed, emotionally or mentally troubled." And the word *soul* means "self." My response to the question the psalmist raises is simple: "I have no one to look to who is greater than myself. Therefore, I am unable to fulfill my own needs and address my own issues."

Have you ever heard the saying, "Everyone has a hole on the inside that only God can fill?" One day that hole inside of me was filled with the Spirit of God, the day when I accepted Christ as my Lord and Savior. Then, the Word of God was able to deliver me from a melancholy spirit, but only my actions helped me to fully experience that deliverance.

One biblical solution to depression is found in Isaiah 26:3: "You will keep him in perfect peace, whose mind is stayed on You" (NKJV). The key to overcoming depression is taking your mind off yourself and diverting it vertically, diverting your thoughts to God, your heavenly Father.

Another solution is seen in the words of Isaiah 41:10: "Fear not, for I am with you; be not dismayed, for I am your God. I will strengthen you, yes, I will help you, I will uphold you with My righteous right hand" (NKJV). The key to overcoming depression is to know you are not alone. Call on God, and He will give you the strength to rise above negative talk.

In addition, Proverbs 3:5–6 instructs us to "trust in the Lord with all your heart, and lean not on your own understanding; in all your ways acknowledge Him, and He shall direct your paths" (NKJV). The key phrase in this Scripture is "lean not on your own understanding." When life is not going the way we think it should go, we tend to produce reasons why. Oftentimes we do not know what is going on behind the scenes of the life we are living. Because of that, we turn inward, bringing on depression and melancholy. When we learn not to lean on our flesh and instead acknowledge God, the Lord Jesus Christ, He will lead us in the way we should go.

Here are other Scriptures to review:

- 1 Thessalonians 5:16 (NIV)
- Proverbs 12:25 (NIV)
- Proverbs 15:13 (NIV)
- Psalm 94:19 (NIV)
- 1 Peter 5:7 (NIV)

So, the solution to depression is hope. Having peace with God gives us hope, and having the peace of God will overcome the hopeless, sad feelings that come to distress us. Hope gives us a future; faith is for today, and hope is for tomorrow.

> *"Have I not commanded you? Be strong and of good courage; do not be afraid, nor be dismayed, for the Lord your God is with you wherever you go."*
> —Joshua 1:9 NIV

DAY ONE
The Hope of Glory

The mystery that has been kept hidden for ages and generations but is now disclosed to the Lord's people. To them God has chosen to make known among the Gentiles the glorious riches of this mystery, which is Christ in you, the hope of glory.

—Colossians 1:26–27 NIV

The mystery is that Christ is in you, and He is the hope of glory. The Old Testament saints did not know about this mystery, but God chose to reveal it to those who accept Christ as their personal Savior. Jesus then sent His Spirit to live within the New Testament Church and to never leave her. In John 14:16–17, He said, "And I will ask the Father, and he will give you another advocate to help you and be with you forever—the Spirit of truth. The world cannot accept him, because it neither sees him nor knows him. But you know him, for he lives with you and will be in you" (NIV; John 16:7 NIV; John 14:20 NIV).

Christ has given Himself to us so we will have the power to live the Christian life. Do you believe that Christ is in you? Is it a mental belief, or does that belief impact your life? *How* does this belief impact your life? Think about it. The Holy Spirit given to the New Testament believers was a mystery in the Old Testament.

The hope of glory is the fulfillment of God's promises to restore us and all creation. The hope of glory includes our resurrection. Romans 8:11 states, "And if the Spirit of him who raised Jesus from the dead is living in you, he who raised Christ from the dead will also give life to your mortal bodies because of his Spirit who lives in you" (NIV).

The hope of glory includes a heavenly inheritance. According to 1 Peter 1:3–4, "In his great mercy he has given us new birth into a living hope through the resurrection of Jesus Christ from the dead, and into an inheritance that can never perish, spoil, or fade. This inheritance is kept in heaven for you" (NIV).

The hope of glory includes a deposit guaranteeing our inheritance: "When you believed, you were marked in him with a seal, the promised Holy Spirit, who is a deposit guaranteeing our inheritance until the redemption of those who are God's possession—to the praise of his glory" (Ephesians 1:13–14 NIV).

God's presence is in the believer. There is a small booklet entitled *Practice the Presence of God* that was written by Brother Lawrence. The book teaches, "God is as present in the kitchen as in the cathedral and as accessible in the living room as He is around the Lord's table. This simple, yet profound teaching will empower you to seek the joy of God's presence during every moment and circumstance."

I began to practice the presence of God in everything I did, and as a result, I would talk to God about everything. It is a habit for me now, to know that God is with me no matter what I find myself doing. I have given away many copies of this book as the Lord leads, to help others also experience the presence of God.

Moses knew the value of the presence of God: "Then Moses said to him, 'If your Presence does not go with us, do not send us up from here. How will anyone know that you are pleased with me and with your people unless you go with us? What else will distinguish me and your people from all the other people on the face of the earth?'" (Exodus 33:15–17 NIV).

Our hope is not in ourselves, but in Christ. Our response should be "thank You for giving us Your Spirit. Thank You for living inside of us. Thank You for never leaving us, nor forsaking us. Thank You for the hope of glory, which is in Christ Jesus."

PRAYER

Write out your prayer.

_____

_____

_____

_____

_____

_____

_____

_____

_____

_____

_____

_____

REFLECTIONS

What are your thoughts about John 14:16–17 (NIV)?

_____

_____

_____

_____

_____

_____

_____

_____

_____

_____

_____

_____

_____

_____

_____

_____

_____

_____

_____

_____

LIFE APPLICATION

Do you believe that Christ lives inside you? If so, when was the last time you thanked Him for this amazing gift?

_____

_____

_____

_____

_____

_____

_____

_____

_____

_____

_____

_____

_____

_____

_____

_____

_____

_____

_____

NOTES

DAY TWO
Hope Deferred

Hope deferred makes the heart sick, but when the desire comes, it is a tree of life.

—Proverbs 13:12 NKJV

Webster's Dictionary describes *hope* as "a state of mind that believes and desires a positive outcome to situations in life." It is a feeling that things will turn out for the best. Another definition of *hope*, called a "spiritual definition," is "a potent and positive practice with the power to pull you through difficult times." It is described as "light," a ray, a beam, a glimmer of hope, the light at the end of the tunnel. We all have heard and even made statements using these metaphors.

The biblical or Christian definition of *hope* is "confident expectation": "But hope that is seen is no hope at all. Who hopes for what they already have? But if we hope for what we do not yet have, we wait for it patiently" (Romans 8:24–25 NIV).

Hope deals with things we cannot see or have not yet received: "Now faith is confidence in… what we do not see" (Hebrews 11:1 NIV). Faith is for today, while hope is for the future. Just as faith upholds us in the here and now, hope sustains us for what is to come. Hope sustains us until we see the fulfillment of our dreams and desires.

Herein lies the issue with the "got to have it now" generation. Instant gratification has no time to wait, and this is how depression sinks in, sadness overwhelms us, and suicide replaces hope. The heart is sick because there is no vision of the future, and there is no confidence in what is to come. We allow our hearts to become sick.

The difference between *Webster's* definition of hope and the biblical definition is our focus. *Webster* talks about feelings and positive thinking. The focus is on self, on the arm of the flesh. "There is no good thing in me, that is, in my flesh" (Romans 7:18 NIV). Your flesh cannot sustain you; in fact, your flesh will drive you to depression and suicide. Our focus must be on the One who has all power and is able "to give you hope and a future" (Jeremiah 29:11 NIV).

Deferred means "to put off, to drag out to a later time, to postpone or delay." Not getting what you want can ultimately break your heart. If you are truthful, you can identify with this statement. Time is a key factor in hope being deferred. While we are waiting, we can experience disappointment and the loss of hope, and this loss of hope can lead to depression, anxiety, and even physical sickness. People without hope see life as meaningless, and this can lead them to lose the desire to live.

Proverbs 13:12 (NIV) says that "a longing fulfilled is a tree of life." That phrase "tree of life" caused me to wonder, *How does desire fulfilled become a tree of life?* As I researched this and while meditating on my findings, I looked back on the fact that hopelessness can bring about death, but hope can bring life and restoration. While we wait, we should turn our thoughts toward God, and when we place our hope in Christ alone, we will not be disappointed. Hebrews 6:19 states, "This hope is a strong and trustworthy anchor for our souls" (NLT). Our emotions, mind, and will must be held in check while we wait.

Young people today need to learn how to have hope, how to overcome despair by resting in God (Psalm 62:5 KJV). Hope changes what we value (Matthew 6:19–21 KJV).

The rewards of hope are found in the following verses of Scripture:

- Psalm 33:18 KJV
- Psalm 31:24 KJV
- Ephesians 2:12 KJV
- Romans 15:4 KJV
- 1 Peter 1:13 KJV
- Colossians 15:6 KJV

May the God of hope fill you with all joy and peace as you trust in him, so that you may overflow with hope by the power of the Holy Spirit.
—Romans 15:13 NIV

PRAYER

Write out your prayer.

_____

_____

_____

_____

_____

Canaan City Limits: Roadblocks Ahead

REFLECTIONS

What are some of the rewards of hope?

_____

_____

_____

_____

_____

_____

_____

_____

_____

_____

_____

_____

_____

_____

_____

_____

_____

_____

_____

_____

_____

_____

LIFE APPLICATION

How has the need for instant gratification affected your life?

_____

_____

_____

_____

_____

_____

_____

_____

_____

_____

_____

_____

_____

_____

_____

_____

_____

_____

_____

_____

_____

_____

NOTES

DAY THREE
My Hope Is in You

And now, LORD, what do I wait for? My hope is in You.

—Psalm 39:7 NKJV

Up to this point, David had lamented his very existence. He was expressing great sorrow and regret about his sin, about his life, and how man walks about like a shadow; in short, he was expressing the vanity of life.

In Psalm 1:1, David starts with these words: "Blessed is the man that walks not in the council of the ungodly, nor standeth in the way of sinners, nor sitteth in the seat of the scornful, but his delight is in the law of the Lord, and in his law does he meditate day and night. And he shall be like a tree planted by the rivers of water; that brings forth his fruit in his season, his leaf shall not wither; and whatsoever he does shall prosper" (KJV). The word *blessed* means "a joyful mental state of contentment; a condition of comfort and security."

As we move through the Psalms, David writes about trusting God; the sinfulness of man; praying for help, confidence, guidance, protection, and deliverance; the wickedness of man; good and evil; and the problem of pain. Then we come to Psalm 39:7, and hope enters the equation. Many of David's observations were personal—all about himself—and yet by verse 7, after all the despair, pain, and wickedness, he wonders what he is waiting for. Then he writes that his hope, his expectation was in the Lord: "Deliver me from all my transgressions: O spare me, that I may recover strength" (Psalm 39:8, 13 KJV).

Like David, so many of us only see our shortcomings. We know we are sinners, and yet we will not acknowledge that we are saved by grace during times of despair. Despair should lead us to our Creator. God should be the end goal of our waiting and hoping. The vanity of earthly things should lead us to hope if we choose to live and not die. Turning to God is our source of consolation. We gain a more cheerful view of life, a comforting view. It is not from what we see in the world; it is not found in our own power—it comes from the God who made all, who is Ruler over all, and who controls all.

> *Whom have I in Heaven?*
>
> —Psalm 73:25 KJV

We should deeply feel the vanity of all earthly things, in order that we may run to God as the Source of all true happiness. If life is a mere shadow, if all is vanity, then what is there to hope for?

Psalm 37:1–7 (KJV) provides us with steps to find hope. Review it and renew your hope in the Lord.

PRAYER

Write out your prayer.

_____

_____

_____

REFLECTIONS

What are some steps to hope?

_____

_____

_____

_____

_____

_____

_____

_____

_____

_____

_____

_____

_____

_____

_____

_____

_____

_____

_____

_____

LIFE APPLICATION

How do you view the world? Be specific.

_____

_____

_____

_____

_____

_____

_____

_____

_____

_____

_____

_____

_____

_____

_____

_____

_____

_____

_____

_____

_____

_____

_____

NOTES

Canaan City Limits: Roadblocks Ahead

DAY FOUR
Hope Does Not Disappoint

Now hope does not disappoint, because the love of God
has been poured out in our hearts by the Holy Spirit who
was given to us.

—Romans 5:5 NKJV

The King James Bible says, "Hope maketh not ashamed" (Romans 5:5), and Psalm 119:116 says, "Let me not be ashamed of my hope" (KJV). So, what determines whether hope leads to disappointment? Hope is a feeling of expectation and the desire for a certain thing to take place. When that thing does not happen, disappointment sets in. The psalmist prayed that God would not let him be ashamed of his hope. In other words, his hope had become a point of shame because he might have been hoping in vain. He prayed that the thing he was hoping would come to pass.

The Bible provides examples of how hope does not disappoint. In Philippians 4:11 Paul wrote, "I have learned, in whatsoever state I am, therewith to be content" (KJV). Although we may have hope for the future, we can be content with what we have now. That contentment is the foundation that will keep you from being disappointed when the outcome is not what you expected.

Paul also wrote: "I know both how to be abased, and I know how to abound: every where and in all things, I am instructed both to be full and to be hungry, both to abound and to suffer need" (Philippians 4:12 KJV). This verse was written by a person who knew how to persevere. When it looks like your hope is in vain, perseverance will keep you from being ashamed or disappointed. Your attitude will be that if your hope comes to fruition, then excellent, but if it does not, you will just continue to wait. Perseverance is persistence in doing something despite difficulty or delay in achieving success.

The same apostle Paul continued to write: "I can do all things through Christ which strengtheneth me" (Philippians 4:13 KJV). Hope does not disappoint when Christ is your strength, and with His help you can patiently wait on the fulfillment of your hope.

And in Romans 8:28, Paul also wrote, "And we know that all things work together for good to them that love God, to them who are the called according to his purpose" (KJV). If we understand and trust in this verse of Scripture, then our hope will never disappoint us. We will never be ashamed of our hope, because we know that all things, good or bad, are working for us because we love God, and we know our purpose in Him.

Frustrated hope fills men with shame and confusion (Job 6:19–20 KJV). Hope is confidence in God's promises. "Having the full assurance of hope" means *being satisfied with what God will be for us and do for us in the future.* Faith, patience, and experience are all wrapped up in the "full assurance of our hope" (Hebrews 6:9–11 KJV).

"For the vision is yet for an appointed time, but at the end it will speak, and it will not lie. Though it tarries, wait for it;

because it will surely come, it will not tarry" (Habakkuk 2:3 NKJV). The vision is the hope you have for the future. Wait for it; it will speak.

PRAYER

Write out your prayer.

_____

_____

_____

_____

_____

_____

_____

_____

_____

_____

_____

_____

_____

_____

_____

_____

_____

REFLECTIONS

Give specific examples of how hope will not disappoint you.

_____

_____

_____

_____

_____

_____

_____

_____

_____

_____

_____

_____

_____

_____

_____

_____

_____

_____

_____

LIFE APPLICATION

Do you have a vision for the future? How long have you been waiting for it to come to pass? Has your hope ever made you ashamed of the vision? Be specific.

_____

_____

_____

_____

_____

_____

_____

_____

_____

_____

_____

_____

_____

_____

_____

_____

_____

_____

_____

NOTES

Canaan City Limits: Roadblocks Ahead

SECTION 7
The Giant of Compromise

- HIVITE: Compromise
- DEFINITION: Mutual concession, yield, combining
- SOLUTION: Jeremiah 18:3–4, 6 KJV

MESSAGE TO THE OVERCOMER

Draw near to God and He will draw near to you. Cleanse your hands, you sinners; and purify your hearts, you double-minded.

—James 4:8 NKJV

Compromise can be positive or negative, depending on the situation. To *compromise* means "to make a deal between two different parties in which each party gives up part of their demand; also, to accept standards that are lower than desirable." Compromise is making concessions to find middle ground. Burke once said: "All government, indeed, every human benefit and enjoyment, every virtue and every prudent act, is founded on compromise and barter."

James 1:6–8 (KJV) says that a person who doubts is like a wave of the sea driven and tossed by the wind. This person is double minded. The term *double minded* comes from the Greek word *dipsuchos*, meaning "a person with two minds or souls." One part of the mind is sure of something, while the other part is not so sure.

So, what do compromise and having a double mind have in common? A double-minded person is always torn in two directions, while a compromiser is always looking for the middle ground. A compromiser is willing to settle for less than the best to play on both sides of the fence. In 1 Kings 18:21, "Elijah came to all the people, and said, 'How long will you falter between two opinions? If the LORD is God, follow Him'" (NKJV).

A double-minded person is one who doubts. On the one hand, he believes, but then doubt comes and tries to share the same space. This is where instability comes into play. Loyalties are divided between God, the world, and self. A double-minded person compromises his values and his faith because he is torn between independence and dependence, having his own way or depending on another, operating in his own strength or leaning on God and depending on His power.

Matthew 6:24 puts it like this: "No one can serve two masters: for either he will hate the one, and love the other; or else he will hold to the one, and despise the other" (KJV). Compromise seeks to find the middle ground, being equally loyal to both masters. Compromise reduces quality and value; it weakens and lowers one's position.

Look at Daniel 1:8 (KJV). Daniel refused to compromise his values by eating food from the king's table. On the other hand, King Saul, in 1 Chronicles 10:13 (KJV), compromised his position with God by seeking counsel from a medium, a familiar spirit, instead of inquiring of the Lord. So, Saul died for the transgression he committed against the Lord.

James 4:4 tells us, "Whosoever therefore will be a friend of the world is the enemy of God" (KJV). Acts 5:29 also says, "We ought to obey God rather than men" (KJV).

In Revelation 3:15–16, the Lord says, "I know your deeds, that you are neither cold nor hot. I wish you were either one or the other! So, because you are lukewarm—neither hot nor cold—I am about to spit you out of my mouth" (NIV). We are looking at one who has chosen the middle ground, one who compromises, one who straddles the fence, one who is double minded. God hates lukewarm Christians. Make a decision—be hot or be cold—but stop straddling the fence, desiring to find pleasure on both sides.

To be single minded means to seek first the kingdom of God (Matthew 6:33 KJV). "Great peace have those who love Your law, and nothing causes them to stumble" (Psalm 119:165 NKJV). Single-minded people have a goal; they clearly see it, and they have visualized themselves claiming it. They will not allow anything or anyone to get in the way of their goal.

When single-mindedness becomes God-centered, it becomes committed, determined to do what God says regardless of cost, focusing solely on pleasing God. When we are sold out to Jesus, we are willing to put our personal agendas aside and focus on doing God's will. Jesus said, "The light of the body is the eye: if therefore thine eye be single, thy whole body shall be full of light" (Matthew 6:22 KJV). Light allows us to see; it gives clarity and the ability to serve God. Every believer is a double-minded Christian on some level, in the process of choosing God over self.

The solution to compromise and a double mind can be found in Jeremiah 18, where we visit the potter's house. Jeremiah saw the potter making something at the wheel, and the vessel he made of clay was marred (ruined) in the hand of the potter; so, he made it again into another vessel. Verse 6 states, "'O house of Israel, can I not do with you as this potter?' says the LORD. 'Look, as the clay is in the potter's hand, so are you in My hand'" (NKJV).

In the potter's process, clay begins as a rock that has to be dug up from the earth and finely ground into dust. Once the dust is carefully combined with other natural substances to develop a pliable material, the potter begins the formation process. The clay is cut, rolled, stretched, pushed, pressed, divided, smashed, beaten, spun, and flipped (Isaiah 64:8 NKJV).

Just as the potter is almost finished, he finds a detrimental flaw that, if not fixed, could destroy the entire piece. The vessel must be taken apart, completely broken so the potter can start the process all over again. The potter does not throw away the clay but reshapes it.

Choose to be in the hand of the Potter so that you may be shaped into a vessel of honor for God's use. Overcome that spirit of compromise; overcome that giant that is trying to keep you from your promise.

DAY ONE
A House Divided

Jesus said, "Every kingdom divided against itself is brought to desolation, and every city or house divided against itself will not stand."

—Matthew 12:25 NIV

Compromise involves making deals, making concessions in the hopes of finding middle ground. As mentioned in the introduction to this section, compromise can be either negative or positive. Whenever there is disagreement between two or more parties, there is sure to be a fallout, especially within families and governments. "Can two walk together, except they be agreed?" (Amos 3:3 KJV). The answer is no. There must be agreement on where the walk will lead. Otherwise, there will be a split, a division, with each party wanting to go in their own direction. Compromise becomes the order of the day, finding middle ground. So, before the walk begins, there should be an agreement on where to go.

Families, husbands and wives, brothers and sisters, and friends all are faced with being divided in their opinions, in their thoughts about how to relate to one another. Every day we are faced with choices to agree or disagree. I once had a friend who disagreed with my theology about salvation. We eventually agreed to disagree for the sake of our friendship. She was always my biggest supporter after that, and she always had my back during those rough times of full-time ministry and living by faith. Without that agreement, without that compromise, without valuing our friendship over the disagreement, I certainly would have lost this good friend.

Divorce rates are high, and one popular reason for divorce is "irreconcilable differences." The legal definition of this is "substantial incompatibility between marriage partners," often called "no-fault divorce." *Merriam Webster* cites this as the "inability to agree on most things or on important things." The heart of the matter is the lack of desire to find middle ground between the two parties. What would you do to make a relationship work? What will you give up because you cannot have your way? Can't we all just get along?

A house divided against itself cannot survive, and it will not stand. All civil war is the result of people not getting what they want. So, they fight for it, kill other people for it, die themselves to satisfy the lust of the flesh, the lust of the eyes, and the pride of life. They fight for their rights, even if their rights violate others' rights.

A house divided against itself is brought to desolation. We see this take place every day. *Desolation* is a state of complete emptiness and destruction. Nations fighting within themselves are destroying homes and businesses, while the inhabitants become refugees looking for a safe place to live. Why? The nations cannot agree on who will rule the area, or they are fighting for religious control.

There is nothing new under the sun. Until Christ is in control, the self will always cause division and strife.

PRAYER

Father,

In the name of Jesus, I thank You for Your Word that comes to heal and to deliver us. I pray that as we understand more and more about compromise and its good and bad sides, we will choose You over all other things that vie for our attention.

I thank You that we, with the help of the Holy Spirit, can avoid civil war within our families and friendships simply by putting others before ourselves. As Christians, we no longer walk after the flesh, after the self-life, but we walk after the Spirit and we desire the Spirit-filled life. Thank You that I can seek my brothers' good and my sisters' good and be in right standing with You.

A house divided is weak, and these individual houses that are Your temples are divided and weak. Thank You for helping us to walk in agreement with You first and with our neighbors second.

I love You, and I desire to be on fire for You, not allowing middle ground to pollute my walk with You.

In Jesus' name, amen.

REFLECTIONS

In what areas of your life are you compromising right now? Be specific.

_____

_____

_____

_____

_____

_____

_____

_____

_____

_____

_____

_____

_____

_____

_____

_____

_____

_____

_____

_____

LIFE APPLICATION

What are you willing to do to make a relationship work? Be honest with yourself.

_____

_____

_____

_____

_____

_____

_____

_____

_____

_____

_____

_____

_____

_____

_____

_____

_____

_____

_____

NOTES

Canaan City Limits: Roadblocks Ahead

DAY TWO
God's Promises
Are Yes

For no matter how many promises God has made, they
are "yes" in Christ. And so through him the "Amen" is
spoken by us to the glory of God.
                          —2 Corinthians 1:20 NIV

As I was writing this section about compromise, I began to wonder, *What does promise have to do with compromise?* To *promise* is "to make an oath," while to *compromise* means "to settle differences." To *promise* is "to commit to something" while to *compromise* is "to bind by mutual agreement."

Another meaning of the word *compromise* is "to expose or to make vulnerable, to make an unfavorable concession or indulgence, to weaken." Here we can see the negative aspect of compromise. If we remove *com* from the word *compromise*, we have the word *promise*. As children of God, we have been given so many promises in the Bible. We often compromise what God has intended for us to enjoy the pleasures of this world. We were made for the promises of God, which lead us to an abundant life!

According to John 10:10, "The thief's purpose is to steal and kill and destroy. My purpose is to give them a rich and satisfying life" (NLT). The purpose of the thief, the enemy, is to cause us to compromise, to make unfavorable decisions that will weaken our relationship with God. He wants us to lose out on the benefits of the promise. He wants us to feel defeated when we compromise our position with God.

Sarah and Abraham were promised a child in their old age. Neither of them could imagine that God would cause it to come to pass. What happened next? Sarah decided to compromise, to find some middle ground, to make God's promise more believable. She weakened His promise by having the arm of man step in and bring the promise to pass (Genesis 16, 21).

How do we compromise the following promises?

- "I will instruct you and teach you in the way you should go; I will guide you with My eye" (Psalm 32:8 NKJV). We compromise by leaning on the arm of flesh. We look to man to instruct us.

- "And we know that all things work together for good to them that love God, to them who are the called according to his purpose" (Romans 8:28 KJV). We compromise by not believing the Word of God, and we don't believe because we only quote the first part of this verse and never realize that the second part is what makes the first part work.

- "If any of you lacks wisdom, let him ask of God, who gives to all liberally and without reproach, and it will be given to him" (James 1:5 NKJV). We compromise this verse simply by not doing what it tells us to do: Ask God! We ask everybody else for their wisdom concerning our problems, but only God gives us as much wisdom as we want ("liberally").

The prefix *com* means "with; together," and it tends to make a word negative. So, how do we compromise the promises of God? We try to help Him with their fulfillment. We put ourselves into the mix, "together" with God, thinking we can make it happen. Our responsibility is to agree with the promise and walk it out. We must agree with a hearty "amen": "Yes, Lord, Your servant hears!"

PRAYER

Father,

In the name of Jesus, thank You for all Your promises we have at our disposal. Thank You for being able to agree with You and Your Word. Thank You for Deuteronomy 31:8 (KJV), in which You promised to go before me and to be with me; You will never leave me nor forsake me. My heart says yes.

In 1 John 1:9, You said, "If we confess our sins, he is faithful and just to forgive us our sins, and to cleanse us from all unrighteousness" (KJV). My heart says, "Yes, Lord, I will confess—say the same thing as You say— and receive forgiveness."

Father, thank You for showing me how to agree with Your promises and how to walk them out to avoid the stumbling block of compromise.

Thank You for all these things, in Jesus' name. Amen.

REFLECTIONS

How has compromise weakened your relationship with God?

_____

_____

_____

_____

_____

_____

_____

_____

_____

_____

_____

_____

_____

_____

_____

_____

_____

_____

_____

_____

_____

LIFE APPLICATION

What promises of God have you compromised or tried to help God bring to pass? Be specific.

_____

_____

_____

_____

_____

_____

_____

_____

_____

_____

_____

_____

_____

_____

_____

_____

_____

_____

_____

_____

_____

NOTES

DAY THREE
Just a Little Bit

A little yeast works through the whole batch of dough.
—Galatians 5:9 NIV

We are still discussing the issue of compromise. How does leaven (yeast) fit into this topic of compromise? First, yeast is a substance that makes dough rise, that puffs it up. Yeast has two primary functions in baking: to increase the volume of the dough and to improve its flavor. Leaven has both a positive and a negative connotation in Scripture.

Jesus mentions leaven in Matthew 16:6. He warned His disciples to "take heed and beware of the leaven of the Pharisees and the Sadducees" (NKJV). The disciples did not understand this metaphor at first, but Jesus helped them to understand that the leaven was the doctrine of the Sadducees and Pharisees. What was their doctrine? The Pharisees were adding man-made rules and regulations to the Scriptures, while the Sadducees were taking away from Scripture by denying the supernatural.

It is dangerous to add or subtract from the Scriptures. Deuteronomy 4:2 clearly states, "You shall not add to the word which I command you, nor take from it" (NKJV; also see Revelation 22:18–19 NKJV).

Compromise can be like leaven or yeast. Remember, compromise means finding a middle ground by accepting standards that are lower than desirable. In compromising what God has commanded in Scripture, you open the door for a little error, for a little sin, and it soon magnifies into something bigger. You may tell yourself it is not so bad, but then corruption has infiltrated your life. Leaven can represent both moral and spiritual corruption.

Compromise usually requires a small token of your desire to play both sides against the middle. Just two steps to the left, staying close to the truth. Just a little bit, so it does not look wrong, but, in fact, it will corrupt the remaining truth. Just a little bit of leaven added to a new lump of dough (a new Christian, a new church member) will cause it to rise and get puffed up—so a little bit of compromise affects your character, and your trustworthiness is no longer valid. The leaven has worked its way throughout. A little bit of leaven infiltrates the entire lump of dough.

According to Matthew 13:33 (KJV), the kingdom of heaven is like leaven, covered up, hidden in the flour, deposited in one place, working silently throughout until all the mass is brought under its influence.

PRAYER

Oh, my God,
Thank You for caring enough about me to show
me what leaven can do to my life. Compromise is like
leaven, and if I compromise my values, I will undoubt-
edly affect the values of someone else. Compromise is
subtle but extremely dangerous, and I thank You for
keeping me on the straight and narrow, guiding me
with Your eye.

Father, in the name of Jesus, teach us more about adding and taking away from Your Word. Help us to live according to the Word You have given us and not allow man to add stipulations to how we walk with You, how we talk with You, and how we treat our brothers and sisters. Thank You for the supernatural nature of Your Word.

In Jesus' name. Amen.

REFLECTIONS

Do you see leaven and compromise as similar agents? Explain your answer.

_____

_____

_____

_____

_____

_____

_____

_____

_____

_____

_____

_____

_____

_____

LIFE APPLICATION

Have you ever tried to make Scripture say what you want it to say by adding or taking away from it? Explain.

_____

_____

_____

_____

_____

_____

_____

_____

_____

_____

_____

_____

_____

_____

_____

_____

_____

_____

_____

_____

NOTES

DAY FOUR
Stand Firm

Be on your guard; stand firm in the faith; be courageous;
be strong.

—1 Corinthians 16:13 NIV

The Clark commentary puts it this way: "Hold in conscientious credence what you have already received as the truth of God." Our faith is so important to the lives we live. When life takes its best shot at us, we need to remind ourselves of who we are in the faith. Otherwise, we become discontent, and we start doubting God and ourselves. Then self, the flesh, the world, and the devil will step up to the plate and offer us a way out through compromise.

If we can learn to encourage ourselves during rough times, we will better be able to overcome the temptation to take life into our own hands. We know there is no good thing in the flesh; we know the devil comes to steal, kill, and destroy; we know all that is in the world is the lust of the flesh, the lust of the eyes, and the pride of life. We know all these things, and yet we still allow the enemy of our souls and our own lustful desires to entice us into compromise.

We need to watch and be on guard. Pay attention to your circumstances. Never allow life to just happen to you. Stay in the Word of God. Meditate on the Word day and night so that your spirit may be strengthened. Our spirit man is in touch with the spirit realm and is able to make us aware of what is happening all around us.

STANDING STRONG

Let no corrupt communication proceed out of your mouth.

—Ephesians 4:29 KJV

Walk in a manner worthy of the Lord.

—Colossians 1:10 KJV

What does the LORD require of you but to do justly, to love mercy, and to walk humbly with your God?

—Micah 6:8 KJV

Trust in the LORD with all your heart.

—Proverbs 3:5 NKJV

Seek ye first the kingdom of God.

—Matthew 6:33 KJV

Do not be conformed to the world.

—Romans 12:2 KJV

Do everything without grumbling or arguing.

—Philippians 2:14 NIV

If we confess our sins, he is faithful.

—1 John 1:9 KJV

*Commit your works to the L*ORD.

—Proverbs 16:3 NKJV

Be strong in the Lord.

—Ephesians 6:10 KJV

PRAYER

Father,

In the name of Jesus, I thank You for helping me stand against the giant of compromise. I can only make my stand on Your Word. Thank You that I am hiding Your Word in my heart, which allows me to speak it forth in my hour of need. Thank You for the stand I am making for You, the stand I am making to encourage others.

Father, I need Your Word more than ever to be able to stand in this world, which is falling more and more into compromise. Nations desire control over the people in such a way as to kill and destroy their own cities. People all over the world are wanting their own way, wanting what they want and wreaking havoc. Governments are wanting control, while every day people are crying out to You for change.

Lord God, I thank You that my trust is in You, and only You. Great and mighty God, great in counsel and in deed, nothing, nothing, absolutely nothing is impossible for You.

In Jesus' name. Amen.

REFLECTIONS

What stood out the most for you in this teaching about standing strong?

_____

_____

_____

_____

_____

_____

_____

_____

_____

_____

_____

_____

_____

_____

_____

_____

_____

_____

LIFE APPLICATION

Choose one of the verses on standing strong and write it out below in a version you like.

_____

_____

_____

_____

_____

_____

_____

_____

_____

_____

_____

_____

_____

_____

_____

_____

_____

_____

_____

_____

_____

_____

NOTES

Canaan City Limits: Roadblocks Ahead

SUMMARY
Encouragement from Others

WEEK ONE:
THE GIANT OF FEAR
Fear Opposes Faith

"The presence of fear does not mean you have no faith. Fear visits everyone but make your fear a visitor and not a resident."

—Max Lucado

"Faith is like radar that sees through the fog—the reality of things at a distance that the human eye cannot see."

—Corrie Ten Boom

WEEK TWO:
THE GIANT OF CARNALITY

The Flesh Wars against the Spirit

"God will never tell us to do something that gratifies the flesh."

—Charles Stanley

"The spirit in the believer's spirit penetrates and spreads throughout their whole inner being."

—Henry Hon

WEEK THREE:
THE GIANT OF DISCOURAGEMENT

The Discouraged Need Peace

"The difference between discouragement and encouragement is who you listen to. God or man."

—David Ibiyeomi

"As we pour out our bitterness, God pours in His peace."

—F.B. Meyer

WEEK FOUR:
THE GIANT OF PRIDE
Pride Opposes Humility

"A person wrapped up in himself makes a small package."

—Harry Emerson Fosdick

"Humility is the displacement of self by the enthronement of God."

—Andrew Murray

WEEK FIVE:
THE GIANT OF
LACK OF DISCIPLINE
The Undisciplined Need Temperance

"An undisciplined life never leads to progress."

—Craig Groeschel

"Temperance is simply a disposition of the mind which binds the passions."

—Thomas Aquinas

WEEK SIX:
THE GIANT OF DEPRESSION
Depression Robs Us of Hope

"The iron bolt which so mysteriously fastens the door of hope, and holds our spirits in gloomy prison, needs a heavenly hand to push it back."

—C. H. Spurgeon

"Hope means expectancy when things are otherwise hopeless."

—Gilbert L. Chesterton

WEEK SEVEN:
THE GIANT OF COMPROMISE
Compromise Is Middle Ground

"Whatever you compromise to gain, you will lose."
—Dr. Myles Munroe

"The provision is in the promise."

—Derek Prince

IN CLOSING

Do not be overcome by evil, but overcome evil with good.

—Romans 12:21 NKJV

"He who overcomes shall inherit all things, and I will be his God and he shall be My son."

—Revelation 21:7 NKJV

About the Author

Rosita Dozier is a native of Little Rock, Arkansas, currently living in Corona, California. She began writing in her preteens; poetry was her outlet. Her poems were about the environment in which she lived and her desire to learn what was beyond the sky and to discover the meaning of life.

Rosita's life changed on August 7, 1981, when she gave her life to Christ. That event set her on a path of studying and learning all that she could about God and His Son, the Lord Jesus Christ. The first six years were set aside for intensive spiritual training and discipleship under the teaching and pastoral ministry of Robert E. Smith Sr., pastor of the Word of Outreach in Little Rock, Arkansas. This training included learning how to pray and study the Scriptures, outreach, teaching, and full-time ministry. The overall focus of the training was to overcome the world, the flesh, and the devil. Thus, living the overcoming life is more than a concept to Rosita; it is a way of life.

Rosita was ordained by Pastor J. Faraja Kafela, who was later ordained as a bishop. She served with him in ministry for five years at Imani Temple in Pomona, California. She also served for seven years under the leadership of Rev. Dr. Charles Lee-Johnson at Corona Community AME Church, and she currently serves with him at The Life Church Riverside. Teaching women is her top priority; she conducts Bible studies and has been teaching about living the overcoming life for over thirty years.

Rosita has drafted articles for church newsletters, helped pastors put oral messages into print, and edited and formatted several books by a local pastor for publishing. She has authored two books that are available at Barnes and Noble and Amazon. Her first book, *There Is a Message to the Overcomer*, was published by Xulon Press, and her second book, *From the Farmhouse to a Powerhouse: An Overcomer's Journey to the Double Portion*, was published by Christian Faith Publishers. Her third book, *Life on Lockdown: Pandemic Expressions*, was published by Rhema Alive and is available on Amazon.

Rosita writes often and looks forward to penning many more books to the glory of God.

Other Titles

A Message to the Overcomer is a collection of messages written to encourage Christians to experience a deeper life in Christ. Each message offers a practical approach to overcoming life's issues. As we apply the word in our lives, we will begin experiencing the overcoming life. My desire is to see God's people grow in grace and in the knowledge of the Lord Jesus Christ. "And they overcame him by the blood of the Lamb and by the word of their testimony, and they did not love their lives to the death." Revelation 12:11 KJV

From the Farmhouse to a Powerhouse is about the transition from a natural life into a supernatural life, a transition from natural power to a double portion of God's power. *Transition* means "changing from one state, position, or condition to another." The first transition we should make is from an unbeliever to a believer in Christ. Then we should transition from a new Christian to a mature Christian, from walking in the flesh to walking in the Spirit, from being overcome to being an overcomer, from having the need for a teacher to being a teacher, from always asking for prayer to being a prayer warrior.

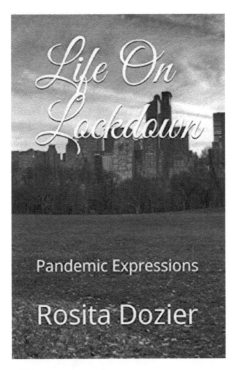

Pandemic Expressions

Rosita Dozier

What if "living on lockdown" is not meant to be an oppression, but rather an opportunity for the world to "get right" with God and one another? What if this "lockdown" is God being merciful, giving us a "time out" instead of a "time's up"? What if this "lockdown" is exactly what we need to become what God created us to be? Of course, most will believe in their hearts that "they don't deserve to be on lockdown," as they hold more lofty ideas of themselves and their actions than they should. Instead of possessing a contrite heart, they, like Pharaoh, will have hardened hearts that only bring greater calamity and suffering.

9 798887 382906